TEXT AND TEXTURE: PATTERNS OF COHESION

Sally Stoddard

Volume XL in the Series
ADVANCES IN DISCOURSE PROCESSES
Roy O. Freedle, Editor

ABLEX PUBLISHING CORPORATION
NORWOOD, NEW JERSEY

OHIO UNIVERSITY
LIBRARY

Copyright © 1991 by Ablex Publishing Corporation

All rights reserved. No part of this publication may be reproduced, stored in a retrieval system, or transmitted, in any form or by any means, electronic, mechanical, photocopying, microfilming, recording, or otherwise, without permission of the publisher.

Printed in the United States of America

Library of Congress Cataloging-in-Publication Data

Stoddard, Sally
    Text and texture—patterns of cohesion / Sally Stoddard.
      p. cm. — (Advances in discourse processes)
    Includes bibliographical references (p.) and indexes.
    1. Cohesion (Linguistics) 2. Discourse analysis. I. Title.
    II. Series.
P302.2.S76 1990
401'41—dc20   90-1190
                                                                                        CIP

Ablex Publishing Corporation
355 Chestnut Street
Norwood, New Jersey 07648

For Bob, Martha, Drew, and Hugh

and for my mother whose curiosity never died.

Table of Contents

List of Figures	*vii*
List of Tables	*viii*
Preface to the Series	*x*
Preface	*xiii*

1	**THE NATURE OF TEXTURE IN TEXTS**	1
	The Dynamics of Texts	1
	The Texture of Texts	4
	The Patterns of Texts	6
	A Definition of Text	9
2	**THE NATURE OF COHESION**	13
	A Definition of Cohesion	13
	The Perception of Cohesion	20
	Research Hypotheses	29
3	**ANALYZING PATTERNS OF COHESION**	32
	Selection of Cohesion Types for Analysis	32
	Selection of a Corpus	45
	Selection of a Reader-Subject	47
	Designing a Computer Program	48
4	**COHESION AS A COMPONENT OF TEXTURE**	54
	The Incidence of Cohesion	55
	The Relativeness of Cohesion	61
	The Visual Patterning of Cohesion	67
5	**COHESION PATTERNS AND TEXTURE IN TEXTS**	92
	Evaluating the Methodology	93
	Evaluating Text as Process	97

Evaluating the Results — 100
Implications of Cohesion and Texture in Texts — 102
The Perspective of Texture — 106

References — 108

Appendix A LIST OF TEXTS ANALYZED — 117

Appendix B LIST OF ABBREVIATIONS USED IN TABLES A–T — 120

Appendix C EXCERPT FROM SNOBOL4 COMPUTER PROGRAM — 131

Author Index — 133

Subject Index — 137

List of Figures

3.1.	Reader-marking of Text for Computer Input	50
3.2.	Map Spacing of Nodes and Cohesive Elements	53
4.3.	Bead-string Model	69
4.4.	Network Model	69
4.5.	Lakoff 1, *Language and Woman's Place*	72
4.6.	Skinner 1, *Beyond Freedom and Dignity*	73
4.7.	Skinner 2, *Beyond Freedom and Dignity*	74
4.8.	Friedman, "Why the American Economy is Depression Proof"	75
4.9.	White, "Once More to the Lake"	76
4.10.	Milford 1, *Zelda*	77
4.11.	Sandburg 1, *Abraham Lincoln: The Prairie Years*	78
4.12.	Sandburg 2, *Abraham Lincoln: The Prairie Years*	79
4.13.	Clark 2, *The Ox-Bow Incident*	80
4.14.	Hemingway 1, *For Whom the Bell Tolls*	81
4.15.	Hemingway 2, *For Whom the Bell Tolls*	82
4.16.	Faulkner, "Dry September"	83
4.17.	Porter, "The Jilting of Granny Weatherall"	84
4.18.	Overlay of Cohesion Maps for Faulkner, "Dry September"	91

List of Tables

4.1.	Number of Nodes Relative to Length of Text (in %)	56
4.2.	Number of Cohesive Elements Relative to Length of Text (in %)	57
4.3.	Number of Unfulfilled Cohesive Elements Relative to All Cohesive Elements (in %)	60
4.4.	Cohesion Index—Nonfiction	63
4.5.	Cohesion Index—Essay	63
4.6.	Cohesion Index—Biography	64
4.7.	Cohesion Index—Novel	65
4.8.	Cohesion Index—Short Story	65
4.9.	Summary Cohesion Index	67
A.	Occurrences of Definite Articles—Nonfiction	120
B.	Occurrences of Definite Articles—Essay	121
C.	Occurrences of Definite Articles—Biography	121
D.	Occurrences of Definite Articles—Novel	122
E.	Occurrences of Definite Articles—Short Story	122
F.	Occurrences of Pronouns—Nonfiction	123
G.	Occurrences of Pronouns—Essay	123

H.	Occurrences of Pronouns—Biography	*124*
I.	Occurrences of Pronouns—Novel	*124*
J.	Occurrences of Pronouns—Short Story	*125*
K.	Occurrences of Agent Displacements—Nonfiction	*125*
L.	Occurrences of Agent Displacements—Essay	*126*
M.	Occurrences of Agent Displacements—Biography	*126*
N.	Occurrences of Agent Displacements—Novel	*127*
O.	Occurrences of Agent Displacements—Short Story	*127*
P.	Cohesion Index Factors—Nonfiction	*128*
Q.	Cohesion Index Factors—Essay	*128*
R.	Cohesion Index Factors—Biography	*129*
S.	Cohesion Index Factors—Novel	*129*
T.	Cohesion Index Factors—Short Story	*130*

Preface to the Series

Roy O. Freedle
Series Editor

This series of volumes provides a forum for the cross-fertilization of ideas from a diverse number of disciplines, all of which share a common interest in discourse—be it prose comprehension and recall, dialogue analysis, text grammar construction, computer simulation of natural language, cross-cultural comparisons of communicative competence or other related topics. The problems posed by multisentence contexts and the methods required to investigate them, while not always unique to discourse, are still sufficiently distinct as to benefit from the organized model of scientific interaction made possible by this series.

Scholars working in the discourse area from the perspective of sociolinguistics, psycholinguistics, enthnomethodology and the sociology of language, educational psychology (e.g., teacher-student interaction), the philosophy of language, computational linguistics, and related sub-areas are invited to submit manuscripts of monograph or book length to the series editor. Edited collections of original papers resulting from conferences will also be considered.

Volumes in the Series

Vol. I.	Discourse Production and Comprehension. Roy O. Freedle (Ed.), 1977.
Vol. II.	New Directions in Discourse Processing. Roy O. Freedle (Ed.), 1979.
Vol. III.	The Pear Stories, Cognitive, Cultural, and Linguistic Aspects of Narrative Production. Wallace L. Chafe (Ed.), 1980.
Vol. IV.	Text, Discourse, and Process: Toward a Multidisciplinary Science of Texts. Robert de Beaugrande, 1980.
Vol. V.	Ethonography and Language in Educational Settings. Judith Green & Cynthia Wallat (Eds.), 1981.
Vol. VI.	Latino Language and Communicative Behavior. Richard P. Duran (Ed.), 1981.
Vol. VII.	Narrative, Literacy and Face in Interethnic Communication. Ron Scollon & Suzanne Scollon, 1981.
Vol. VIII.	Linguistics and the Professions. Robert J. DiPietro (Ed.), 1982.
Vol. IX.	Spoken and Written Language: Exploring Orality and Literacy. Deborah Tannen (Ed.), 1982.

Vol. X.	Developmental Issues in Discourse. Jonathan Fine & Roy O. Freedle (Eds.), 1983.
Vol. XI.	Text Production: Toward a Science of Composition. Robert de Beaugrande, 1984.
Vol. XII.	Coherence in Spoken and Written Discourse. Deborah Tannen (Ed.), 1984.
Vol. XIII.	The Development of Oral and Written Language in Social Contexts. Anthony D. Pellegrini & Thomas D. Yawkey (Eds.), 1984.
Vol. XIV.	What People Say They Do With Words. Jef Verschueren, 1985.
Vol. XV.	Systemic Perspectives on Discourse, Volume 1: Selected Theoretical Papers from the 9th International Systemic Workshop. James D. Benson & William S. Greaves (Eds.), 1985.
Vol. XVI.	Systemic Perspectives on Discourse, Volume 2: Selected Applied Papers from the 9th International Systemic Workshop. James D. Benson & William S. Greaves (Eds.), 1985.
Vol. XVII.	Structures and Procedures of Implicit Knowledge. Arthur C. Graesser & Leslie F. Clark, 1985.
Vol. XVIII.	Contexts of Reading. Carolyn N. Hedley & Anthony N. Baratta (Eds.), 1985.
Vol. XIX.	Discourse and Institutional Authority: Medicine, Education, and Law. Sue Fisher & Alexandra Dundas Todd (Eds.), 1986.
Vol. XX.	Evidentiality: The Linguistic Coding of Epistemology. Wallace Chafe & Johanna Nichols (Eds.), 1986.
Vol. XXI.	The Acquisition of Literacy: Ethnographic Perspectives. Bambi B. Schieffelin & Perry Gilmore (Eds.), 1986.
Vol. XXII.	Cognitive and Linguistic Analyses of Test Performance. Roy O. Freedle & Richard P. Duran (Eds.), 1987.
Vol. XXIII.	Linguistic Action: Some Empirical-Conceptual Studies. Jef Verschueren (Ed.), 1987.
Vol. XXIV.	Text and Epistemology. William Frawley, 1987.
Vol. XXV.	Second Language Discourse: A Textbook of Current Research. Jonathan Fine (Ed.), 1988.
Vol. XXVI.	Systemic Functional Approaches to Discourse. James D. Benson & William S. Greaves (Eds.), 1988.
Vol. XXVII.	Language Development: Learning Language, Learning Culture. Ruqaiya Hasan & James Martin (Eds.), 1989.
Vol. XXVIII.	Multiple Perspective Analyses of Classroom Discourse. Judith L. Green & Judith O. Harker (Eds.), 1988.
Vol. XXIX.	Linguistics in Context: Connecting Observation and Understanding. Deborah Tannen (Ed.), 1988.
Vol. XXX.	Gender and Discourse: The Power of Talk. Alexandra D. Todd & Sue Fisher (Eds.), 1988.
Vol. XXXI.	Cross-Cultural pragmatics: Requests and Apologies. Shoshana Blum-Kulka, Juliane House & Gabriele Kasper (Eds.), 1989.
Vol. XXXII.	Collegial Discourse. Allen D. Grimshaw, 1989.
Vol. XXXIII.	Task, Talk, and Text in the Operating Room: A Study in Medical Discourse. Catherine Johnson Pettinari, 1988.
Vol. XXXIV.	The Presence of Thought. Introspective Accounts of Reading and Writing. Marilyn S. Sternglass, 1988.
Vol. XXXV.	Japanese Conversation: Self-contextualization through Structure and Interactional Management. Senko Kumiya Maynard, 1989.
Vol. XXXVI.	Cognitive Assessment of Language and Matho Outcomes. Sue Legg & James Algina (Eds.), 1990.

Vol. XXXVII.	Pragmatics, Discourse and Text: Some Systemically-inspired Approaches. Erich H. Steiner and Robert Veltman (Eds.), 1988.
Vol. XXXVIII.	Conversational Organization and its Development. Bruce Dorval (Ed.), 1990.
Vol. XXIX.	Developing Discourse Practices in Adolescence and Adulthood. Richard Beach & Susan Hynds (Eds.), 1990.
Vol. XL.	Text and Texture: Patterns of Cohesion. Sally Stoddard, 1991.
Vol. XLI.	Conversation Analysis of a Marital Therapy Session: The Pursuit of a Therapeutic Agenda. Jerry Edward Gale, 1991.
Vol. XLII.	Medical Discourse and Systemic Frames of Comprehension. Ronald J. Chenail, 1991.
Vol. XLIII.	What's Going On Here? Complimentary Studies of Professional Talk. Allen Day Grimshaw et al., 1991.
Vol. XLIV.	Ambiguous Harmony, Family Talk in America. Hervé Varenne, 1991.
Vol. XLV.	American and Japanese Business Discourse: A Comparison of Interactional Styles. Haru Yamada, 1991.
Vol. XLVI.	Scientific Discourse: An Analysis of Biomedical Journal Articles' Discussion Sections. Betty Lou DuBois, 1991.
Vol. XLVII.	Repetition in Discourse: Interdisciplinary Perspectives, Volume 1. Barbara Johnstone (Ed.), 1991.
Vol. XLVIII.	Repetition in Discourse: Interdisciplinary Perspectives, Volume 2. Barbara Johnstone (Ed.), 1991.
Vol. XLIX.	Word Choice and Narration in Academic Lectures: An Essay on Artistic Language Use. Barbara Strodt-López, 1992.

Preface

Once a semester I put a standard 750ml green wine bottle on the desk in front of my freshmen composition students. They were usually curious, of course, but skeptical when I asked them to "Draw the wine bottle." Inevitably the pictures, copied onto the blackboard, were relatively alike:

Like the many students before them, none used his or her power to imagine the bottle from a different angle:

Yet, until we have exhausted all the perspectives from which we can view phenomena in our world, we will not understand what those phenomena are all about.

With this lesson in mind, my research on the relationship of texture, pattern, and cohesion in written texts began to take shape. It was evident to me that readers derive much more meaning from their reading than the sum of the words printed on the page. In other words, readers create textual synergism. This holistic phenomenon has largely been ignored in the literature on discourse processes, probably because of its overwhelming complexity. Nevertheless, it is a phenomenon that can be explored, even at this "primitive" stage of our research.

The perspective of this book begins with the claim that the perception of synergism is due in part to the texture of a text and that texture, in turn, is composed of various kinds of text patterns. One type of pattern is created by cohesive ties. By exploring the nature of and variations in these patterns of cohesion, both numerically and visually, I suggest that a holistic view of texts is possible and merits further investigation.

The premises and results of this study did not come about in a vacuum. The earlier work of many thinkers referred to throughout the book is evidence of this. I received continuing encouragement for my ideas from numerous sources. I am especially indebted to Julia Penelope who has always been supportive of unconventional points of view. Paul Kramer, who is an ingenious geographic computer expert, wrote the plot program which made the text maps possible. Roy Freedle, Sharad Seth, Bob Haller, Paul Olson, and Les Whipp contributed valuable suggestions at critical points. Bob Stoddard not only suffered the slings and arrows of outrageous fortune at the supper table, but was a critical reader of more than one version of this book, giving a valuable outsider's point of view. Additional colleagues and friends cheered me on for which I will be eternally grateful.

1
The Nature of Texture in Texts

THE DYNAMICS OF TEXTS

A text is a phenomenon of seemingly infinite complexity because of its synergistic nature. This synergism allows us to derive meaning which is exponentially greater than the sum of the lexical meanings in texts and greater than the sum of the sentential meanings. This is true because textual synergism is realized in the mind as we construct texts. In other words, the dynamics of synergism are not isomorphic with a linear, sequential text. One cause of the multidimensionality of synergism is a global component which can be referred to as "texture."

Component sentences of a text, which in themselves are structures of intricately woven form and meaning, are subject to global properties, such as texture, which greatly increase our interpretive potential. One of the rudiments of texture is cohesion, a type of unifying device which we construct, consciously or unconsciously, as we process texts. It is this characteristic, as it contributes to texture and the dynamic nature of texts, which is examined here.

However, singling out one text component, such as cohesion, risks oversimplifying the complex nature of texts and perpetuating reductionism. The problem for linguists in this regard is not unlike that of other scientists who set as their goal an explanation of the whole by analyzing "basic" units and assuming that they somehow "add up." Indeed, it is symptomatic of a problem affecting the larger scientific community—a problem of dogmatic tunnel vision, well-stated by Ashby:

> Science stands today on something of a divide. For two centuries it has been exploring systems that are either intrinsically simple or that are capable of being analyzed into simple components. The fact that such a dogma as 'vary the factors one at a time' could be accepted for a century, shows that scientists were largely concerned in investigating such systems as allowed this method; for this method is often fundamentally impossible in complex systems. (1964, p. 5)
>
> . . . There are complex systems that just do not allow the varying of only one factor at a time—they are so dynamic and interconnected that alternation of one factor immediately acts as cause to evoke alternations in others . . .Until re-

cently, science tended to evade the study of such systems, focusing its attention on those that were simple and especially, reducible . . . (1964, p. 60)

Because of the types and numbers of variables involved in texts and because of the size of the potential database, we have hardly begun to address the dynamic aspects of texts (Green & Morgan, 1981, p. 168). Certainly sentence grammar models do not and cannot account for textual synergism. We can, of course, continue to look at one or two components of text at a time, but if we do, we must be very honest about the limitations of doing so. Simply describing individual components will not yield a holistic picture of them. Nevertheless, the immensity of the task of accounting for the synergism of texts can easily render our efforts in this direction nugatory and entice us to return to the womb of atomism from which modern linguistics arose—unless we initiate our studies with nontrivial questions based on valid assumptions and seek answers through appropriate methods of analysis. Hrushovski suggests:

> Theory must not shy away from the diffuse, ambivalent, multidirectional, imprecise, potentials-filled nature of language—which is its great strength in interacting with a multifarious and changing 'World.' One should not confuse method with ontology, the neatness of a theoretical apparatus with a schematic neatness in language. (1982, pp. 159–160)

If we set aside our previous conceptions of text and previous methods of analyzing and describing those texts, we will be free to look at other perspectives. Exploring the nature of texts can be an exciting and dynamic process in itself—if we are open to different perspectives[1] and can avoid past short-sightedness.

One far-sighted view is that of Marvin Minsky (1975) whose concept of "problem space" is a research model worth examining. Minsky suggests that in a problem-solving situation—which understanding the notion "text" is—we need to investigate the problem space to find the right questions before we attempt to find "the right answers." He says (1975, p.259):

> The primary purpose in problem solving should be better to understand the problem space, to find representations within which the problems are easier to solve. The purpose of the search is to get information for the reformulation, not—as is usually assumed—to find solutions; once the space is adequately understood, solutions to problems will more easily be found.

According to this view, initial explorations are an attempt to find an appropriate perspective from which to describe the problem and to find a

---

[1] Minsky's (1975) analogy with visual perceptions of a room demonstrates the value of looking at a problem from various angles.

solution. These explorations are not subsequently labeled "success" or "failure," but rather "promising" or "not promising" for future investigation. Seen in this light, the work of most text linguists is valuable, but limited, and can hardly be said to be definitive. What Hrushovski (1982), Minsky (1975), and Schmidt (1977) are saying is that until a text theory is able to account for the dynamic, synergistic aspects of text, it is not a comprehensive, explanatory theory. However, we will not succeed in defining the problem space nor be able to articulate an adequate theory of texts by continuing to construct shot-in-the-dark hypotheses and claiming more explanatory power for them than is warranted.

Before we formulate an adequate theory, we need an understanding of the nature of the problem space "text" which will necessarily include discovering the elements which are common to all texts and those which differentiate texts. To do this, we must change our strategies and adjust our assumptions. For one thing, it is essential that we understand the relationship between text and the complex social milieu of which it is a part. It has become increasingly obvious to researchers testing Transformational theory (e.g., Hankamer & Sag, 1976; Reinhart, 1980) that texts cannot be considered as entities independent of the producer, processor, and environment in which they are generated and received because intuitive "proofs" using contrived input data simply break down when such data are placed in appropriate contexts (Hrushovski, 1982). As Schmidt (1977, p. 51) points out:

> Formal text theories are still far from explaining the functioning of natural languages in social contexts and the mechanisms of social communication processes . . . [A]ll communicative text theories work with unsatisfactory models of action and communication . . . Most . . . are no more than item-collection models . . . without proper specification of the relations between the items.

Unfortunately, many studies (notably Halliday and Hasan's typology of cohesion, 1976, Clark's typology of bridging, 1977, and de Beaugrande's typology of entities subject to the status of definiteness, 1980) fall under "item-collection models." Until our theories and our methods begin to reflect a change in direction away from list making, we will have made little progress in accounting for the synergism of texts.

To change our perspective, we cannot simply consider text as it relates to the writer as producer, the text as product, or the reader as processor; we need to study the interactiveness of these factors in order to understand the notion "text" holistically.[2] Even though not all writers intend their products to be

---

[2] Because the research reported here is limited to written texts, I will couch my arguments accordingly—even though many of them apply to speech as well.

read,[3] as Schmidt (1977, p. 51) says, "[C]ommunicative text theories must be firmly based on the empirical investigation of communication processes." To do so, of course, is to invite continuing, confounding problems which are not immediately solvable because it is not easy to separate texts definitively from the social components with which they are intricately intertwined in ways that we do not yet fully understand. Still, we need to continue to explore all aspects of communication processes both as discrete components to steer us to the "right" questions and as interrelated parts of the whole. The task of defining the problem space "text" justifies limiting research to less than a holism at this stage, but only if we keep in mind the ultimate goal.

THE TEXTURE OF TEXTS

It is the purpose of this study to explore one aspect of that problem space, namely, the notion of "texture," and more particularly, its manifestation in patterns of cohesion in written texts. Texture, in one sense, involves the quality of dimensionality, or depth, which may range from minimal (approximating "flatness") to maximal, or any stage between. This variation in range creates variation in texture. Texture also has to do with the organization of material. In texts, this texture is the result of the overlaying—as it were—of the patterns created by the readers' perceptions of the content, the rhetorical structure, and the linguistic structure of the physical text so that, at any given point in the reading process, the texture may be similar to or different from that at some other point.

An analogy with music will illustrate what I mean. If we listen, for instance, to a Bach Brandenburg Concerto, we may or may not be aware of the recursiveness of themes which at times involves simply the repetitions of notes and chords in particular sequences and at other times involves the intracacies of inversions and mirroring. Yet, as we listen, we are affected in particular ways by this texture. At times passages are dense, intense, colorful, undulating, swirling, and at others, the music is soft, subdued, tremulous, thin, hardly moving. In any case, we feel literally "immersed" in the music which seems to fill the space around us. This dimensionality, this depth and recursiveness, is more than the sequentiality of the notes printed on the sheet of music; it is synergism which is generated by the variety and number of instruments which are playing at any one time, by the relative loudness or softness of the tones, by the harmonic patterns and by our collective experience as we listen. In other words, we perceive certain textures in the music as

---

[3] Certainly not all writers intend to communicate with readers, at least in the sense of allowing readers to understand all the motivations behind the writing (e.g., propagandists), and writers of journals most commonly do not intend their work to be read by other persons at all.

it is played—an experience quite different from simply seeing or playing the musical notes printed on a sheet of paper.

Our encounters with the visual arts likewise provide an example of our experiences of texture. For instance, the delicate transparency of a watercolor miniature on a finely textured paper provides a striking contrast to an oil painting done on a large, rough canvas daubbed with thick layers of ochre and cadmium blue and alizarin crimson paint. These contrasting examples can be combined as mixed media which might well employ an even larger range of textures. Or, we can compare the texture of a monolithic sculpture of highly polished marble, a Michelangelo perhaps, with a bas relief of rough-carved wood. The texture of each of these, in turn, will differ markedly from any of the canvas-oriented arts. Nevertheless, a large part of our understanding of a piece of art is related to our experience of texture as a whole or as a particular segment—an effect which varies with the media, the color, the forms, the technique, and the viewer's experience of art.

Still another textural analogy can be made with the variation of textures in fabrics. We have only to mentally run our hands over fabrics such as corduroy, satin, slub weaves, georgettes, homespun, cable knits, fine silks, and thick woolens to appreciate the range of textures in textiles. The soft downy delicacy of a pashmina shawl contrasts with the varied roughness of a homespun cableknit fisherman's sweater or the sequined tutu of a ballerina. While many of these fabrics—especially those used in clothing construction—have consistent (but not necessarily regular) textures, fabrics constructed to be art pieces may display an even wider variety of textures within one piece such as applique, crewel embroidery, macrame hangings, and modern woven tapestries. These textures are achieved through the variation in fibers, the admixture of colors, the mode of construction, and so on. Our visual appreciation of these textures is often enhanced by our hands-on experiences of them.

If texture is a component of these other arts, then is it not logical to believe that it is also a characteristic of literature? I suggest that it is—that when we read a text, a part of the synergism we derive is contributed by its texture though we may not be aware that this is so. We have no metalanguage to talk about it, but nevertheless we know that at times, as we read, we are caught in the grip of excitement or the depth of an emotional moment while at other times we are passively absorbing information. Sometimes the intensity of a section of a text is so great that, when the moment is over and the writer provides a respite in the form of mere description, or the quiet musing of one of the characters, we welcome the change of pace. Surely it is not simply the typography of the text that captures us so completely, any more than it is the configuration of notes on a sheet of music which absorbs our attention.

One might object that these analogies are vague and defy systematic description, but I believe we can be more precise about the nature of texture, even at this early stage of text research, than we have in the past. I believe this is true because the texture of texts is a composite of patterns—storyline patterns, rhetorical patterns, linguistic patterns and so on—which when overlaid to create the totality of a text create variant textures which are like the "fingerprint" of a text. This texture is more palpable than might be imagined and certainly is not flat, two-dimensional, nor even sequential as physical texts are.[4] I suggest that we actually experience, albeit unconsciously, the repetition and the recursiveness of patterns in a text as they fold back on themselves and entwine themselves around the subject matter. We sense that the texture of Sandburg's *Abraham Lincoln*[5] is different from *The Autobiography of Malcolm X*. Just as Rimsky-Korsakov's "The Flight of the Bumblebee" would not be the same if the patterns of notes were changed or if it were played as a violin solo, so White's essay "Once More to the Lake" would not be the same if it were written in third person as is Friedman's essay "Why the American Economy is Depression-proof." Yet we have not sufficiently explored why this is so.

THE PATTERNS OF TEXT

Only a few linguists have ventured to talk about texture in a meaningful way. Halliday and Hasan (1976) discuss "texture," but it is not at all clear what they mean by it. At one point they seem to equate it with what is traditionally called "coherence," and at other times, they seem to use "texture" as I am using it here. Sedelow and Sedelow (1966, p. 3) also refer to texture but, unlike Halliday and Hasan, claim that it is a "stylistic variable" which is comprised of "tone" and "patterns of word association." Indeed it might be argued that what I am calling texture is no more than what is traditionally called "style." Certainly they are related. A writer may have a particular style which is evident in everything he/she writes, but the texture of a particular text is unique, unlike any other text, even one by the same writer. This is so because writers produce unique sentences and because readers exhibit individuality in their interpretations. The fact that each text has a particular texture, however, does not negate the occurrence and re-occurrence of certain text patterns, part of which are concrete and observable in physical texts. It is the regularity of such patterns that this study explores.

Pattern in a general sense refers to some element which is repeated or which is potentially repeatable, the element itself often being uniquely and

---

[4] I believe this in spite of Winograd's claim that "language is constrained to a primarily one-dimensional medium" (1977, p.66).

[5] References for the texts mentioned in this paragraph are listed in Appendix A.

interestingly constructed. Although pattern is basic to texture, few of the potential text patterns have been systematically described, even though many linguists talk about them. Markels (1983), for one, suggests that "cohesive patterns" and "structural patterns" are textual in nature, rather than being purely linguistic, and Fowler (1981, p. 67) affirms this view saying that cohesion is "linguistic patterning which contributes to the impression that a text 'hangs together.'" Further, Halliday and Hasan (1976, p. 21) claim that "linguistic patterns ... embody, and at the same time impose structure on our experience of the environment ...." Because of this, they suggest, patterns help us to understand a text as coherent and consistent with our knowledge, experience, and environment.

These comments suggest the functions of patterns, but the notion of pattern in texts is so ill-defined that it is difficult to know just what various scholars mean, if indeed they have gone beyond an intuitive sense of what pattern is. Therefore, I want to look more closely at the notion of pattern in language, and particularly as a component of texture in texts, and to look at it from a new perspective.

Traditionally, we have thought of texts as two-dimensional, linear, and sequential, or, in other words, isomorphic with the physical text. Furthermore, we have seen text from a reductionist point of view as deriving meaning from the sum of the several essentially discrete components, but this view obviates the synergism of texts. Hampden-Turner (1981, p.8) states the problem lucidly:

> We "map" with words as well as images but because words come in bits and pieces many people have assumed that the world is in bits and pieces too, with bits corresponding to words ... The idea of linear cause and effect, for example, is inherent in the structure of a sentence, where a subject acts by way of a verb upon an object, but this may be a very inadequate rendering of what is happening, especially of mutual influences. One way to correct this verbal bias is to supplement words with visual maps. If the human mind is to be conceived as a whole as well as parts, we need not just words to convey parts, but patterns, pictures and schemata to convey the whole.

Acknowledging the limitation of using the map concept, however, Hampden-Turner points out that maps "are usually two dimensional" [6] and that "verbal explanations suffer the same limitation" (1981, p. 8).

Unquestionably Hampden-Turner's criticisms are valid, but freeing ourselves from the notion of text as the flat page of the physical text will not be

---

[6] Geographers, of course, have always presented physical land features on three-dimensional models, and more recently have begun using computer graphics to show sociological phe-

easy. If text has a "shape" [7] we do not know what it is, but finding a systematic way to describe texture may help us to understand this amorphous concept.

One factor which must be considered in describing patterns as input to texture is the likelihood of a pattern occurring sequentially or even intermittently over large stretches of text. That is, if patterns repeat only in short spans of text, we would have little basis for believing that texts are a synergistic whole. A part of textual synergy depends on the global potential of patterns which span sentence, paragraph, and even chapter boundaries. Stone (1979, p.9) says:

> A passage of English which is a text has within it certain linguistic features that can be said to link it together or unify it into a whole . . . [and] give it texture.

---

nomena in simulated three-dimensional models. The population map of the state of Nebraska below by Steven Lavin is an example.

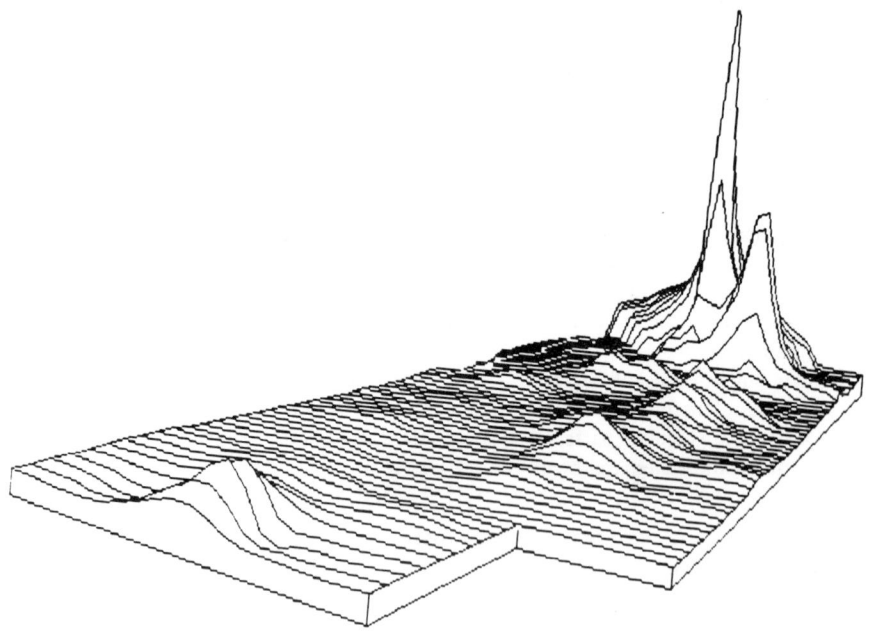

[7] The notion of "shape," of course, is irrelevant if we conclude that texts are linear, sequential, and flat like the physical realization of a text is. However, to stop at such a definition means that we limit our perspective of the problem space and our understanding of texture and textual synergism.

Intuitively we know that such unity of texts does not just happen. It happens because readers perceive the interactiveness of "text components."[8] It is these components that offer the tangible evidence for the limits of the problem space—whatever they are. Because these appear to have a degree of consistency across all texts, they should be identifiable as texture-forming mechanisms. The interactiveness of the patterns generated by these text components constitutes the texture of a text.

A DEFINITION OF TEXT

So far I have been using the term "text"[9] without giving a reasonably satisfactory working definition or characterization of it. While such a definition is crucial to any study of text because it contains basic assumptions made by the researcher, many studies suffer for the lack of it. That this is so is not surprising because the term "text" is not easily defined. Some definitions ignore the synergism of texts and the realities of text processing. For instance, one position in a more traditional linguistics mode appears to claim that texts can be investigated and explained in isolation from their environment as the "physical realization of some semantic unit of discourse" (Kantor, 1977, p.6) or "a concrete and analyzable linguistic entity . . . spoken or written . . ." (Simmons, 1979, 10). These definitions are attractive because they imply communication and because the physical text is the most concrete entity available to us for analysis. However, we know that if we reread passages, we rarely interpret them exactly the same way the second time, or even the third. Thus, our perceptions of text meaning are not unchangeable. Because this is true, we know that a "text" is not a static entity (as is a physical text). A "text" is more than the tangible realization of a physical text.

A more philosophical perspective is that of Fowler (1981, p.21) who suggests that a text is "the mediation of a set of ideas using forms of expression drawn from one, or more usually, more than one, variety/ies." This position acknowledges text as the relating of ideas to linguistic forms, which implies "the writer writing." Similarly, Dijk (1977a, p.5) claims:

> At one level of description, a text is simply an ordered sequence of propositions, which under various pragmatic, stylistic, and other constraints is mapped onto a sequence of sentences.

---

[8] Actually, components are not discrete entities but continuous and interactive. In a sense, it is deceptive to try to study them as discrete.
[9] The terms "text" and "discourse" are often used interchangeably. I use "text" because it seems to be less often applied to oral expression while "discourse" seems to be applied more often to oral expression.

This view suggests that a writer produces and orders propositions which are transcribed as a physical text within constraints applied by the writer.

Other researchers have also considered text as production. These studies are largely related to teaching composition (e.g., Witte & Faigley, 1981; Markels, 1983; Fahnestock, 1983; Bamberg, 1983; Stotsky, 1983; Moskovit, 1983). However, analyzing the production process of already-published texts is an almost impossible task because it is rare that even a research scholar is privy to the mind of the writer of a particular text,[10] and so such studies, when undertaken, must remain inconclusive. We can and do conjecture, of course, about the way a particular text is written and "what the writer had in mind" but we can rarely be confident, except in an intuitive way, whether we are "right" or not. Thus, defining text as writer-oriented is as problematic as defining it as the equivalent of some physical realization.

Yet another and even more complex notion of text which does acknowledge the communicative purpose of texts is that of de Beaugrande and Dressler (1981, p. 3) who define text as "a communicative occurrence which meets seven standards of textuality [cohesion, coherence, intentionality, acceptability, informativity, situationality, and intertextuality]." What they mean by "a communicative occurrence" is crucial here. If they mean that the "conduit metaphor"[11] is valid—that ideas can, in fact, be transferred from one person to another in toto—then writer intent and reader interpretation should coincide perfectly. However, Green and Morgan (1981, p. 177) reject the conduit metaphor citing a reader's pragmatic competence to interpret a physical text as evidence that his/her mental model of a text may be and most often is different from that of the writer of the text.

Certainly, a study of text processing by readers can be more easily undertaken in a systematic manner than the study of a writer's processes (as evidenced from both a writer's perceptions and the texts they produce). Studies of the reading process are numerous (e.g., Clark, 1975; Clark & Carlson, 1981; Clark & Haviland, 1977; Webber, 1980, 1981), but we still know very little about the complexities of the mind or just how the eye-brain combination attends to and understands printed texts. Unfortunately, readers' metaperceptions of their own reading processes are probably as difficult to access as a writer's metaperceptions of his/her writing, except that we can conduct tests that give us clues to readers' processes.

One of the most carefully considered definitions of text is that of Halliday and Hasan (1976) whose disparate statements are summarized below. They say a text is a passage of discourse which is:

---

[10] Some writers are long since deceased, of course, but some are not conscious of their own productive processes and may not want to be made conscious of them. Some may simply not want to apprise others of these inner processes. In any case, introspection is not wholly reliable.

[11] Reddy (1979) discusses the implications of the conduit metaphor at some length.

- a semantic, not a grammatical unit
- encoded in sentences, but not structurally related to them
- related to context of situation by a consistency of register
- reasonably homogeneous and thus consistent across all texts
- characterized by certain linguistic features which are the basis of cohesion in the text and thereby give it texture
- not defined by size.

This definition seems to separate form from meaning which, on the face of it, seems anathema to a holistic view of text. Nevertheless, it does acknowledge the difference between the notion "text" and the physical text and implies the elements in a communication situation.

None of these definitions, however, accounts for the varibility of interpretation by readers of a written text (by either one reader on several readings of the same text or by more than one reader of the same text). The only way to do so is to consider a "text" to be a state of mind. For the writer, a text is a mental model, the product of his/her thinking and intentions (insofar as these can be consciously expressed). This might be called a "writer's text." Few writers, however, would claim that the physical texts they produce are a perfect realization of their mental model. Also, a writer may construct many mental texts which are never transcribed in physical text form. Only when a realization of a writer's text appears in tangible form do readers have access to the producer's ideas.

Readers, in turn, construct their mental models[12] of "text" as they are reading words on a page. This might be called a "reader's text." Just how closely a reader's text coincides with the writer's can only be estimated, but we do know that readers will work hard to construct "text" out of what they read. Indeed a text probably exists if readers want to believe it does. Halliday and Hasan (1976, p. 54) claim that:

> The hearer [reader] typically assumes that any passage which for external reasons *ought* to be a text (as opposed to something that he knows to be a fragment, such as one end of a telephone conversation) *is* in fact a text; and he will go to enormous lengths to interpret it as complete and intelligible.

A reader's text, then, is the reader's mental reconstruction of a writer's text that is not available except through some physical representation of the writer's ideas; neither can it exist without what Green and Morgan (1981, p. 168) call the processor's "interpretive competence" to construct a reasonable mental model (however comparable to the writer's it may be). Because there

---

[12] Both Webber (1980, 1981) and Green and Morgan (1981) describe the reader's role in interpreting a text as a mental model.

are many readers for every physical text and because they can be assigned certain tasks to test their interpretations and because their interpretations do account for the synergism of texts, I believe that this definition of a reader's text is the only one that adequately addresses the realities of text processing. This definition is fundamental to this research.[13]

With this definition in hand, then, we can consider more specifically how patterns of cohesion operate in written texts to contribute to the textual synergism perceived by readers. Chapter 2 establishes the parameters of cohesion in texts and sets forth the hypotheses which guided the research.

---

[13] Because we so often use the term "text to refer to the physical, typographical realization of the writer's mental model, I use the term in that sense where I refer to the written works analyzed for cohesion. I could adopt a typographical convention such as consistently using all capital letters to spell one of the versions of the word, but I have rejected this option assuming that the context makes the usage clear.

2
The Nature of Cohesion

A DEFINITION OF COHESION

Cohesion, one of the many text-forming devices, is easily perceived but not easy to define. One reason for this difficulty is that cohesion is often confused with another of the text-forming mechanisms, namely, "coherence." If cohesion and coherence can be said to have some degree of discreteness (and it is questionable whether any text component can be described as totally independent of the others), the unique characteristics of each and their relationship must be as carefully defined as possible. This is not a simple task as some attempts at definition will illustrate.

One of the primary disagreements among discourse analysts is the question whether these concepts are linguistically determined or contextually determined. Eiler (1983, p. 169), for instance, describes cohesion as an evaluative measure of texts by which we judge a text to be "a good or bad text . . . a mediocre or highly successful text." She seems to think of cohesion contextually as an aid in literary criticism rather than as a linguistic device (or else she is defining it very broadly). Her thinking contrasts with that of Reinhart (1980) who sees cohesion as quite simply "the overt linguistic devices for putting sentences together [which comprise] connectedness [in a text]" (p. 163) or "linear concatenation" (p. 167). For her, cohesion is evidenced linguistically, especially in referential links and sentence connectors, and is one of the conditions of coherence which she defines as:

> A set of norms or conditions which apply to a (perhaps idealized) subset of the set of comprehensible actual or producible texts . . . which observe maximally, or ideally, the requirements of rationality and cooperation, or that reflect the speaker's knowledge of what counts as a freely coherent text. (Reinhart, 1980, p. 161)

She sees coherence as a type of well-formedness in texts determined by the speaker, global in nature, and comprising the "semantic and pragmatic relations in the text" (p. 163).

Like Reinhart, Fredericksen (1977, p. 314) believes that cohesion is a component of textual coherence, but he also believes that cohesion "has to do with the manner in which a discourse relates to what is being said in a current sentence to knowledge which is presupposed, either within the text . . . or outside the text." Accordingly, coherence is "the property that makes a discourse more than a collection of unrelated simple sentences."

In direct contrast to Reinhart and Fredericksen, Markels claims (1983, p. 450) that coherence is a function of cohesion. Her reasoning for this comes from composition textbooks. She says:

> Cohesion embraces the traditional textbook notion of coherence as connections among adjacent sentences and the notion that these local connections must produce a sensible whole.

Markels continues that "coherence as traditionally produced by repetitions and transition words is not always commensurate with a unified, sensible whole" (1983, p. 450). Thus, it appears that Markels reverses Reinhart and Fredricksen's use of the terms "cohesion" and "coherence".

Other scholars see the relationship between cohesion and coherence still differently. De Beaugrande and Dressler claim that cohesion is one of the standards of textuality and that it "concerns the way in which the components of the surface text . . . are mutually connected within a sequence . . . [in] grammatical dependencies" (1981, p. 3). They claim that coherence has to do with the "ways in which the components of the textual world, i.e. the configuration of concepts and relations which underlie the surface text, are mutually accessible and relevant" (where a concept is related to cognitive content and relations link concepts).[1] Thus, de Beaugrande and Dressler appear to be claiming that cohesion and coherence are somehow related to surface structure form and content respectively. That is, they seem to be divorcing form from meaning which appears to contradict their definition of text as a "communicative occurrence" (p. 10).

Because Halliday and Hasan (1976) have been very influential in the discussion of cohesion, their understanding of what constitutes cohesion is worth examining. In the first place, it is puzzling that they do not define coherence. This is the more surprising in that it is a ubiquitous term in the literature concerned with texts. Does this mean that they do not believe there is such a concept, whatever it may be called? Probably not. Rather, it appears that most of the functions of the concept as often defined have been subsumed by Halliday and Hasan under their term "texture," as was mentioned earlier (p. 11).[2] In contrast, they are much clearer about their view of "cohesion." The following are the characterizing elements which Halliday and Hasan ascribe to cohesion (as I have summarized them).

---

[1] To whom the configurations are accessible and relevant, they don't say.
[2] Carrell (1982) agrees with this view of Halliday and Hasan's position.

- Cohesion is a semantic concept (not a structural one) which is concerned with meaning relations in a text and "interrelates the substantive meanings of the text with each other [but does not concern] what a text means" (p. 26).
- Cohesion occurs "where the *interpretation* of some element in the discourse is dependent on another" (p. 4) because one presupposes the other so that each pair of dependent/independent elements creates a "cohesive tie."
- Cohesion may be indicated by either grammatical signals or by vocabulary; that is, by specific linguistic features and lexical expressions.
- Cohesion is a component of "texture" along with the relations which hold between the language of the text and "the relevant features of the material, social and ideological environment" (p. 20).
- Cohesion is a "relation" in the system as well as the "set of possibilities" in the language which the writer (producer) can utilize to make the text hold together. But cohesion is also a "process": the "instantiation of this relation in a text." The latter is directional in that a text, according to Halliday and Hasan, is sequential in real time; the former is without direction (pp. 18-19).
- The presence of cohesion is generalizable to all texts regardless of genre.

Several points are not clear here. For instance, how can cohesion be "a semantic relation" without concerning "what a text means"? Can a concept such as cohesion be narrowly semantic? And, what or who causes the "instantiation" of the cohesion relation in the text? Can a writer "make the text hold together"? Even if a writer utilizes all the cohesive devices available, does it mean that the reader will perceive a text as "cohesive"? In spite of these and other questions, there is much here that is intuitively acceptable as well. This definition is the basis for Halliday and Hasan's typology of the grammatical signals and lexical possibilities which are made available to the processor by the producer.

However, even this complex of defining statements does not address all the problematic aspects of cohesion (as perhaps none will soon). If coherence and cohesion are valid text components—and the consensus seems to be that they are—why is there so much confusion about them? A major reason is that texts are considered the milieu of several disciplines, such as the four I have outlined below with their varied approaches. This means that research in each of these areas, while overlapping to some extent, has a particular perspective—and a particular bias. Although the characterization here is simplistic, the discussion will suggest why scholars have arrived at their divergent positions regarding cohesion.

Theoretical linguistics. This position attempts to describe and explain the grammar of a language. It assumes that the grammar of a language is adequate to characterize the nature of texts. It also assumes that a text, as a language object, can be studied "objectively" in isolation from a communicative environment. Grammaticality can be judged without reference to the way language users create and process texts.

In this case, cohesion is deemed to be present if a physical text contains appropriate syntactic signal-bearing lexical items indicating their semantic relationship with some other part of the text.[3]

Philosophy. This position assumes that linguistic expressions in a physical text "refer" to an object outside the text (in the "real world") or to a mental reality. Because the context of this perspective is the cultural milieu (i.e., philosophical orientation) of the producer and processors, a text is a product of the group for which the objects and mental representations in the text exist as reality. In this view language is the vehicle for expressing the relationships which hold among such objects and mental realities, including cohesive relationships.

From this second perspective, cohesion might be said to occur if elements within a text clarify such relationships, and if language users are thereby able to derive "meaning" from the text in relation to the culture.

Psychology. The context in which texts are studied by psychologists is the human brain and its language-processing function. This view is concerned with the writer's encoding of an intended message in appropriate language and with the reader's decoding of that message. Readers decode the physical text by processing that which is explicit, by using their memories of preceding text and their general knowledge to process that which is implicit, and by making inferences as needed to construct a reasonable interpretation.

According to this view, if the mind of the processor makes appropriate mental associations using physical text input both directly and with additional inferences either consciously or unconsciously, the perception of cohesion is the result.

Pragmatics. This position, predicated on the speech act,[4] takes into account Grice's Cooperative Principle (1975) that (a) writers have a benign intent in writing, and (b) readers intend to cooperate. This means that a writer must estimate what and how much readers know at any given point in the reading process and produce a discourse which is of interest to and interpretable by readers. This also means that readers interpret texts according to their ability with a desire to construct a model of the text which is as close to that of the writer's as possible.[5]

In this pragmatics model, cohesion occurs if the writer provides adequate

---

[3] This position precludes the notion of lexical cohesion as Halliday and Hasan (1976) describe it because repetition, lexical substitutions, and some conjunctives would be considered stylistic choices and hence not in the purview of theoretical linguistics as traditionally conceived.

[4] For a fuller treatment of speech act theory as it impinges on text, the books by Sadock (1974) and Bach and Harnish (1979) are valuable.

[5] Readers' strategies in the interpretation process are little understood though the studies on miscue analysis by Kenneth and Yetta Goodman (e.g., 1977) report research on this question.

textual guidance to readers and readers believe their interpretations of meaning relationships indicated in the text are appropriate and similar to those of the writer.

It is obvious that narrow disciplinary perspectives of cohesion, as outlined above, force researchers in these disciplines to disagree about the nature of cohesion in written texts. A holistic view of cohesion, and consequently texture, must be based on elements common to all the perspectives (i.e., that which is valid in each). One of these is the existence of a linguistic expression (in the physical text) which bears a syntactic clue, either explicit or implicit, signaling the need for a particular kind of mental processing. It is what I call a cohesive *element*. In other words, this cohesive element is marked, whether explicitly or implicitly, to be associated in a particular meaning relationship with another linguistic expression which I call a cohesion *node*. The association itself can be called a cohesive *tie*. A set of cohesive elements tied to a single node form a *network* (Halliday & Hasan, 1976). The networks form patterns of cohesion. (Although Halliday and Hasan, 1976, cite lexical choice, or vocabulary, as a type of cohesion, it is not considered here as such because the processing is of a different nature than syntactically marked types.)

Actually, however, it is not accurate to speak of cohesion as being wholly "in" the physical text. A naive processor might well attribute the perceived cohesive ties to the presence of linguistic signals in the physical text,[6] but cohesion is more complicated. Since we know that readers interpret written texts variously, cohesion cannot be said to exist on the printed page which never varies. It could be either a mental construct of the producers of texts or of the processors of those texts. Some might argue that cohesion is only the former (i.e., created by the writer) and insofar as a text satisfies the writer's intent to create cohesion, this is true but we seldom have access to this information. Even though well-intentioned writers may allow for what they believe to be a cohesive, interpretable text, only the processors can confirm whether writers have succeeded in giving them sufficient, interpretable clues to construct cohesive ties. We must conclude that *cohesion* is a mental construct resulting from reader processing.[7]

If it is true that cohesion is a function of text processing by the reader, then to assume that cohesion can be analyzed from physical text input only is misguided. In fact, linguistic signals indicate no more than the *potential for cohesion* until readers associate elements with appropriate nodes—which some of them may or may not do because they have different processing abilities, they read sloppily, or they do not bring adequate experiences to their understanding of text material. This is to say that if cohesive elements and their nodes exist in the physical text and a reader does not interpret the

---

[6] This tendency points up the problems of doing perception studies.

[7] Although the theoretical perspective above appears to disallow this view, even the notion of "contextual restrictions" would be invalid if there were no producers or processors of language.

cohesive tie (for whatever reason), cohesion cannot be said to exist at that point for that reader even though another reader may well make a suitable connection and judge it cohesive.

Nevertheless, in spite of the potential for differences of interpretation by various readers, if cohesion is a valid component of discourse, we can predict that most native speaker readers will have little difficulty establishing cohesive ties—especially if, in the great majority of instances, potential cohesive ties are available and are available unambiguously in the physical text.

However, it is not always easy to make these connections. One instance is that of ellipsis which according to Halliday and Hasan (1976) is one of the categories of cohesive types. It may seem counterintuitive to claim that ellipsis, the deliberate "leaving out" of some linguistic element, can be cohesive, but as Leech and Short (1981, p. 247) point out: "Cohesion frequently involves the principle of *reduction,* whereby language allows us to condense our messages, avoiding the repeated expression of ideas." To avoid redundancy by employing ellipsis means the deleting of a "second mention" where the "first mention" is present in the physical text. In this case, a cohesive tie must obtain between the first mention and the structure where the ellipsis is employed. The cohesion in such an instance will depend on the reader's ability to infer what has been deleted—a process ordinarily carried out so unconsciously that most readers probably do not realize they do so. Nevertheless, the necessity for inferred cohesion does exist and may or may not be easy to process unambiguously.

It is obvious in this and other situations that cohesion is not *inherent* in a physical text; only the potential for it is. Whatever cohesion exists *in* a text exists because a reader perceives certain meaning relationships which are triggered by the physical text and based at least in part on explicit or implicit syntactic signals. Still, it is useful to talk about linguistic expressions as having cohesive potential, and I believe we should have no hesitation in doing so as long as we are clear that cohesion does not inhere in typographical conventions but rather is created by the mind of a reader.

A cohesive element and its associated node, then, as Halliday and Hasan (1976) have suggested, constitute a cohesive tie. A set of ties having a single node constitutes a network of cohesion. Such a tie, or connection, demonstrates that cohesion is an interface of syntax and meaning where the syntax facilitates the meaningful interpretation of a text by a reader. In this sense, Reinhart (1980) is correct in asserting that cohesion is a kind of "semantic" connectedness.[8] Minsky (1975, p. 231) reinforces this view by saying:[9]

---

[8] There is good reason to prefer "meaningful" in this case although Reinhart uses "semantic."
[9] Minsky (1975, p. 232) also points out that larger structures of linguistic activity are more likely to "blur the distinctiveness of the syntax-semantic dichotomy" than sentence-level analyses can show.

Since the meaning of an utterance is "encoded" as much in the positional and structural relations between the words as in the word choices themselves, there must be processes concerned with analyzing those relations in the course of building the structures that will more directly represent the meaning . . .

Cohesion is one of these processes. No doubt cohesion interrelates with other text-creating components which also interface syntax and meaning (e.g., given/new, topic/comment, and information focus), and these relationships are not trivial, but their complexities at this stage proscribe their discussion here.[10]

If, then, cohesion is a product of reader-processing which interfaces syntax and meaning, how does it differ from coherence? There are several points to be considered. In the first place, coherence is also a reader function, but it does not involve the same kind of processing as cohesion because it is not primarily dependent on syntactic elements as is cohesion.

Coherence partially depends on whatever meaningful relationships are interpretable from the cohesive ties in a text but it is more than these. Coherence is the totality and unity of "sense" in a text. Cohesive ties may be local (within the same clause or same sentence) or global (across sentence or paragraph boundaries), but for the most part, the potential for cohesion is strictly intratextual.[11] Coherence, on the other hand, is definitely global in nature. In fact, coherence is not only global intratextually, as de Beaugrande and Dressler (1981), Reinhart (1980) and others suggest; it also includes the connection between the text and the cognitive and experiential environment of the processor. In fact, it is possible that, even though the potential for cohesion exists in a physical text and readers may identify cohesive ties within a written passage, they may not judge the text to be coherent. That is, in texts such as the following simplistic contrived example, there are cohesive ties easily interpretable across sentence boundaries, but they cannot be said to form a coherent text:

Abraham Lincoln lived in Illinois. This Midwestern state rejected the Equal Rights Amendment to the U. S. Constitution. It is the basis for the laws of our land.

An extreme example like this illustrates that our minds will work hard to "comprehend" a text and still find that it lacks coherence. Reinhart (1980, p. 162) says:

---

[10] Such studies as that by Markels (1983) do consider such relationships.

[11] An example of this is the case of a text which is sprinkled with unfamiliar Latin quotations which are not translated for the reader. The reader may well be able to figure out most of the cohesive connections otherwise but not find the text coherent for lack of understanding the Latin.

An analysis of text-coherence which does not make this distinction between coherence (a type of well-formedness) and comprehensibility will not be a theory. It would amount to endless lists of cohesive devices that have appeared in actual, examined, comprehensible texts.

That this is so is evident, for instance, when we try to read some text that is esoteric to our particular orientation to the world.[12] While we might find various parts of the text cohesive and comprehensible, we might not find the text coherent. This means that comprehensibility is a function of cohesion and that cohesion is distinct from coherence. Still, coherence is far more difficult to describe and explain because it is proposition-related, and we have little understanding as yet of how we "construct" meaning. (Hrushovski [1982], and Green and Morgan [1981], discuss this issue rather compellingly.) Both coherence and cohesion are text-forming components, but cohesion is far more accessible to us because it operates on direct syntactic evidence.

THE PERCEPTION OF COHESION

Cohesion, then, is a mental construct, the result of readers associating cohesive elements in a physical text with appropriate nodes. Although very little research has been done on readers' perceptions of cohesion,[13] I would suggest that certain factors inherent in the nature of cohesion will affect their perceptions. One general category of these has to do with certain characteristics of cohesion which are available to the reader in the physical text because of the writer's input. Another has to do with reading strategies.

The Influence of the Writer

To a certain extent cohesive patterns are affected by a writer's choices in producing a physical text, whether these choices are conscious or not. If a writer did not choose to make certain cohesive elements and nodes available in certain locations in the physical text, readers could not perceive ties. Once nodes and elements have been written into a physical text, however, the patterns of cohesion perceived by a reader are affected by at least six properties of cohesion: number, distance, directionality, re-entry, intersection and type.

Number of Cohesive Ties. The first of these is the relative number of available cohesive elements and nodes. That is, the greater the number of

---

[12] A nonnative speaker unfamiliar with idioms in a target language are a case in point. An idiom may be comprehensible literally (as in "Kick the bucket" in English) but, if that person doesn't know the idiom, the text may not be coherent for that person.

[13] Garnham (1987) is an exception.

potential ties per node a writer makes available, the more unified we would expect readers to perceive the text to be and the more palpable the texture because a larger network will affect a larger portion of the text. Considered otherwise, if each node had only one tie, there would be little cohesion and little texture developed from cohesive ties.

Distance. The second factor is that of the distance spanned by each cohesive tie, that is, the physical text distance between each node and each of its elements. Theoretically, the distance between the ends of ties may vary from nothing to full textlength. The aggregate and the average distances are a function of this distance.

Halliday and Hasan (1976), in their extensive typology of cohesive types, include distance in their discussion of the characteristics of cohesion, but they do not address the power of distance in influencing the perception of cohesion. The studies by Witte and Faigley (1981) and Clark and Sengul (1979) indicate readers are better able to interpret cohesive elements when they are close to their nodes. Reinhart (1980, p. 167) believes that for cohesive conditions to apply, "the distance between the sentences [containing the ends of cohesive ties] cannot be too big."

These discussions tempt us to gloss over the importance of distance as a factor in textual unity and texture. While short ties are easier to interpret, they add little to the overall unity of a text. Distance, of course, is easy to ignore if an analysis includes only short segments. Indeed, if writers observed only adjacent-sentence cohesion rules or even within-paragraph rules, they would risk producing a written text which readers would find to be at least minimally cohesive but not coherent. If all ties were of minimal length (such as within the same sentence), readers might well perceive the texture to be "uninteresting."

Directionality. A third aspect of cohesion to be considered is directionality which is concerned with word order. In this case, it is the position of the cohesive element relative to its node (when an appropriate node is present in the physical text) that is important. If a linguistic expression marked with a cohesive signal occurs at some point in the physical text following its node, the cohesive element is considered to be *anaphoric* or "pointing back."[14] If, on the other hand, a linguistic signal points in the other direction (i.e., to something which follows it), it is *cataphoric*.

Some linguists do not consider cataphora to be cohesive, however.[15] Halliday and Hasan, for instance, claim that personal pronouns are "normally cataphoric only within a structural framework, and therefore do not contribute to the cohesion of the text" (1976, p. 56) and that "*the* can never refer

---

[14] Not all linguists use the term "anaphoric" in this way. For instance, Hankamer and Sag (1976, p. 394) see anaphora as a phenomenon related to deep and surface structures, or in other words, not related to text.

[15] Cataphoric pronouns and their nodes appear to occur only intrasententially and thus contribute minimally to cohesion. For this reason, they may be considered as noncohesive perhaps.

forward cohesively. It can only refer to a modifying element within the same nominal group as itself' (1976, p. 72). However, if we understand cohesion to depend on reader processing—that is, readers making associations between cohesive elements and their nodes—then a cohesive element may occur either preceding or following its node because cohesion can occur if the reader's expectation is eventually fulfilled.[16] But there is no reason to believe (in spite of Halliday and Hasan) that such an association—even within a structural unit such as an expanded noun phrase—is less valid as an instance of cohesion simply because it is thus positioned.[17] In fact, a reader encountering a cohesive element for which a prior node is not available may very well hold it in abeyance assuming that it is cataphoric and will be fulfilled eventually. Stone (1979, p. 70) claims:

> readers will continue to process unrelated bits of information in the hope of locating information in the text that will organize the information they are holding in the presently overburdened memory buffer . . .

There are, of course, instances of definite noun phrases at the beginning of texts for which a logical node does not follow immediately or even later.[18] In this case, it is simply unfulfilled just as others may be that occur later in texts. Nevertheless, I believe that both cataphoric and anaphoric cohesion can and do occur, though instances of cataphoric pronouns are relatively rare.

Reentry. Networks of cohesion display not only number, distance, and direction but also the potential for showing patterned repetition as well. That is, the very repetition of cohesion networks, and especially those with identical nodes, creates similar patterns and thus unity which contributes to texture. For instance, a writer can choose to remention a character by name several times (reentry)[19] with only one or two cohesive elements (e.g., pronouns) tied to each mention, or he/she can use the name only once so that all other mentions are cohesive elements. In the case of the former, the distance spanned by the ties will be relatively shorter than those in the latter, and the perceived patterns and resulting texture will be different.[20]

---

[16] Studies by Green and Morgan (1981), Schank (1978), and Goodman and Goodman (1977) are pertinent here.

[17] Halliday and Hasan (1976) do not consider definite noun phrases such as *the creeping vines of ivy and wild grape* to be cataphoric, but I do, and the data are marked accordingly.

[18] Such cases involve unfulfilled cohesion which is discussed below.

[19] The whole question of a writer's decision to "reenter" either a particular cohesive element or a node into a text is an interesting topic. Jordan (1983), Bolinger (1979), and Grimes (1975) have useful insights into the reentry question.

[20] An example of this is Hemingway's repeated use of Robert Jordan's name in segment 1 compared to a single entry node in segment 2 of *For Whom the Bell Tolls* which is discussed in Chapter 4.

Intersection. Another aspect of writer-influenced cohesion patterns is the case where networks overlap one another as opposed to being spatially separated. Intersecting patterns are logically more complex. On the one hand, this suggests that they require more complicated mental processing. On the other hand, it suggests that, because there is apparently more cohesion present, the cohesion networks may require less processing.

Type. Halliday and Hasan's typology (1976) sets out identifiable types of cohesion. Not all of them are interchangeable, but some are. Where they are, the writer's choice may have an effect on a reader's perception, for instance, choosing an epithet with a definite article instead of a pronoun and vice versa (e.g., "the grandmother"/"she") or choosing one conjunctive rather than another (e.g., "although" for "but"). While these involve lexical choice on a writer's part, they may also have syntactic and semantic implications which might affect the perceived texture of a text. Three types of cohesion are discussed in detail in Chapter 3.

It is writers who determine the possibilities of occurrence, distance, directionality, reentry, intersection, and type. Without this potential, there would be no reader-perceived texture in texts.

The Input of the Reader

While the various aspects of cohesion described above can be predicted to affect readers' perceptions of cohesion, other factors may also affect the success with which readers interpret physical texts. That is, if cohesion is to "occur" (a connection is to be made in the reader's mental model, the way readers process texts will affect their perceptions of cohesive patterns and thus texture.[21]

Three theories which provide insights into reader processing are relevant. The first concerns the way readers organize knowledge. The second and third are concerned with the interaction of readers and physical texts.

Frame Theory. The first of these theories concerns what Marvin Minsky calls a *frame* which he describes as a model for representing the organization of knowledge in the mind.[22] Minsky (1975, p. 212) says:

---

[21] While studies have been carried out with readers as subjects, such as that by Clark and Sengul (1979), none has approached the problem of cohesion in written text processing of extended lengths. Clark and Sengul, for instance, investigated how readers process given/new information by studying the way they identify referents. There are several problems with their study, however. For one thing, subjects were presented with only one sentence at a time in writing, when in reality readers would ordinarily be able to reread at will. Furthermore, their three-sentence "context paragraph" is probably insufficient to understand how readers process text components which span larger chunks of text.

[22] While others have adduced variations of Minsky's model using such terms as schema (Norman & Rumelhart, 1975), scripts (Schank & Abelson, 1977), domains of interpretation

> When one encounters a new situation (or makes a substantial change in one's view of the present problem), one selects from memory a substantial structure called a frame. This is a remembered framework to be adapted to fit reality by changing details as necessary. . . . A *frame* is a data-structure for representing a stereotyped situation . . . We can think of a frame as a network of nodes and relations [collections of which] are linked together into frame systems.

Minsky envisions each frame node[23] as having a variable number of *terminals* which are concepts associated with the frame node in a stereotypical environment. Each terminal has a default value which is triggered when the frame node is referred to—unless a new value is brought into the picture to replace a particular default value. This theory adds the element of context to the underlying semantic representations of frame nodes and terminals.[24]

According to frame theory, a person, on encountering information related to a previously entered frame node (i.e., old information or information already known), conducts a memory search for the appropriate frame. If the information is new, the reader may use that new information to either replace a terminal default value or to create a new frame. Sanford and Garrod (1980, p. 470) refer to this procedure as "bottom up" processing. This latter operation is automatically put into play when a new value does not immediately match a terminal already in place or when considerable bridging must occur to associate the new value with an established frame node.

An example will illustrate how frames work. If we have a frame, established from prior knowledge, which is labeled "Abraham Lincoln," it will have terminal values already in place, such as the male personal pronouns (*he, him, his, and himself*), or other terminal values such as "the rail-splitter," "lawyer," "the Sixteenth President," "Honest Abe," and so on. The exact terminal values will vary with the processor's prior knowledge of the frame node.[25] This is borne out in Garrod and Sanford's research (1977) on the

---

(Stenning, 1977), and domains of reference and scenarios (Sanford & Garrod, 1981), I have adopted Minsky's model and terminology.

[23] The term "frame node" in this study is used to refer to Minsky's concepts of a knowledge framework while "node" or "cohesion node" is used to refer to one member of a cohesive tie.

[24] In fact, in exploring the problem space "text," we will eventually discover just how the frame node is related to other text phenomena such as given/new, topic/comment, and information focus.

[25] For example, the proverbial alien from Mars (assuming a humanoid with a brain which operates like ours) would have to establish a new frame "Abraham Lincoln" which initially would have no terminal values except for pronouns. He/she/it would have to begin filling these values in order to communicate with Americans. Foreigners coming to the United States, on the other hand, may already have established the frame node "Lincoln" and have a few terminal values, but may need to adjust these values as well as add new ones as their knowledge of the frame expands.

Conjoint Frequency Effect which shows that, because some terminal values for a particular frame are used more frequently than others, they are more rapidly identified. This would indicate that not all terminals have the same relationship with the frame node. (Gentner's work discussed below further explains this, and Rumelhart's 1977 study confirms this conclusion.)

The frame "Abraham Lincoln" ordinarily will intersect with other frames such as "American presidents," "frontiersmen," "assassinations," and so on.These intersecting, interacting frames create an extremely complex system of interrelationships which need further semantic exploration of the creative type which Hrushovski (1982) speaks about.

Minsky's hypothesis about the representation of knowledge in the mind provides an alternative to previous models for the retrieval of information from memory. One commonly cited model claims that we make a linear search through our memories to find a "referent" to match each "reference" in the same way that a computer searches for information. Clark and Sengul (1979, p. 36), for instance, suggest two different models, the "continuity model" and the "discontinuity model," but both appear to claim a linear search. While such a model of processing is convenient and attractive for its simplicity, it is unthinkable for its inefficiency. In fact, we really have no very clear picture of how the mind does tap into information which is stored in some form in the brain. Frame theory, however, allows us the possibility that information in long-term memory is not stored in chronological (i.e., in order of accessing) or sequential order, but rather is stored in intersecting, interactive frames which are more likely to be "webby" in nature, rather than linear. A three dimensional visual model of molecular structures, for instance, may better suggest how frame networks operate. In any case, Minsky's model frees us to envision the "depth," or texture, of texts.

I believe that frame theory and cohesion are related by an analogous postulate. This postulate says that each cohesion node is a frame node and each cohesive element is a terminal value. This means that, just as there are potentially many terminals for every frame node, so there are potentially many cohesive elements for every cohesion node. From this I would suggest that networks of cohesion are, in fact, frames. By thinking of cohesive networks as frames, we can better account for the reintroduction of particular nodes (frame nodes) in a text, a concept which is discussed further in Chapters 4 and 5. Thus, frames are a convenient conceptual model of the way readers retrieve and process information as they read.

Theory of Anaphoric Hierarchy. The second theory which is pertinent to processing cohesive ties is Lakoff's hierarchy of anaphoric expressions. Lakoff (1976, p. 295) suggests that anaphoric expressions (or, terminal values) can be ranked according to their degree of definiteness from the most to the least definite as follows: (a) proper names, (b) definite descriptions, (c) epithets, and (d) pronouns.[26] The experiments of Garrod and Sanford support Lakoff's notion of varying degrees of specificity. They say (1977, p. 88):

> If the individual is identified through a variety of different terms in the text, the memory location for that individual will be labeled with the most specific of terms . . . The inclusion of such a labeling constraint would explain why it is that sentences identifying an individual with a term more specific than that previously mentioned . . . take substantially longer to read than those using a more general term. . . . In fact, cases where a more specific term is used in an anaphoric phrase are very rare in normal texts, presumably because of such a constraint.

Analogously, to apply this thinking to the frame-cohesion model, we can assume that readers understand that there are varying degrees of familiarity or definiteness in terminal values. There is not a perfect fit, however, and not all readers will evaluate terminals in the same way. For instance, some readers may find that *he,* a pronoun which is of lower rank according to Lakoff, is more readily accessible as a cohesive element referring to the frame node *Abraham Lincoln* than, say, *the husband of Mary Todd,* a definite description. This perception depends on a reader's previous knowledge of Lincoln as a frame node and whatever terminals he/she has associated with that node. While this suggests that Lakoff's hierarchy needs amending to allow for variance in reader knowledge, nevertheless, we sense that Lakoff and Garrod and Sanford are basically right. The notion of varying degrees of specificity may constrain the ease with which readers understand anaphoric expressions in the frame-cohesion model.

The connectivity hypothesis. The third processing theory which is promising as a partial explanation of reader processing of cohesion is the connectivity hypothesis. Like frame theory, it is concerned with the form in which semantic data are stored in the brain for retrieval. Gentner (1981, p. 77) compares it with the complexity hypothesis as follows:

> The *Complexity Hypothesis* is motivated by the "bin" view of memory, in which the capacity limitations of various stages of memorial processing form a central theoretical notion. The *Connectivity Hypothesis* is based on a more structural view of memory, in which the representational assumptions are crucial. The predictions of the *Complexity Hypothesis* derive from considering long-term memory as a limited-capacity storage system. The predictions of the *Connectivity Hypothesis* derive from considering memory as a structured set of concepts and

---

[26] Lakoff (1976), like others concerned with anaphora or with definite articles or with texts, does not define for whom (the producer or the processor of texts) the expression is definite—a point which I believe is crucial in characterizing certain linguistic expressions as "definite" or "indefinite." The section in Chapter 3 on the definite article discusses this further.

relationships, in which greater connectivity between two concepts leads to higher probability of retrieving one concept given the other. Thus the number of semantic components in a representation is an important predictor in the *Complexity Hypothesis* . . . while the structure of representations is crucial in the *Connectivity Hypothesis*. [Emphasis added.]

From this, she cites a general processing principle which underlies connectivity, namely, the "ability to remember one concept given another increases with the number of stored semantic connections between the two concepts" (p. 76). This is amply illustrated by the clues which are given in crossword puzzles; the closer the clue is to a synonym, the easier it is to recall the word. Gentner tested and confirmed the hypothesis by having subjects recall one noun in a context where it is semantically associated with another via an intervening verb (e.g., the agent and patient of a transitive verb). Her results confirm the connectivity hypothesis and its underlying principle.

The connectivity hypothesis appears to fit the frame-cohesion model very well. From it, two analogous postulates of cohesion-frames can be formulated which have direct implications in writer/reader strategies (discussed in Chapter 5). These postulates can be stated as follows:

1. The greater the number of cohesive elements (terminal values) in a text which a reader perceives as being tied (by a semantic relationship) to a single node (frame-node) in a text, the greater is the likelihood that he/she will remember the network-node (frame-node) to which the ties (relationships) are drawn.
2. The greater the number of semantic connectors between each cohesive element (frame terminal value) and its node (frame-node), the greater is the likelihood that the network-node (frame-node) will be remembered.

While none of the analogous postulates formulated here have been tested to my knowledge, they provide insights into the complexities of text-processing. There are undoubtedly mitigating factors that have not been explored, such as intervening networks, but intuitively, we sense that Minsky's Frame Theory, Lakoff's Theory of Anaphoric Hierarchy, and Gentner's Connectivity Hypothesis are valuable resources in examining reader processing of cohesive ties.

Certainly, not all readers process physical texts in the same way or with the same degree of success. As readers construct their individual mental models (i.e., texts), their models or interpretations will vary because their "interpretative competence" varies (i.e., their ability to tap into memory storage and to use appropriate frames).[27] "Interpretation" is used here in the sense of Green

---

[27] Green and Morgan (1981) and Webber (1980, 1981) discuss such mental models of texts.

and Morgan (1981, p. 168) who say the "interpretation" of a text is "the process of arriving at an understanding of a text," or the attempt to derive meaning from a text. This notion is different from what is commonly referred to as "literary interpretation." They further clarify this differentiation by saying:

> Critical analysis can also involve inferences about text that go far beyond what the author intended; this seems to us an entirely different matter from the interpretive abilities involved in simple comprehension of the text. (1981, p. 170)

Instances in which a reader cannot or does not find an appropriate node for every cohesive element in the available data illustrate the relativeness of this ability in the perception of cohesion.[28] They are special cases of reader processing. That is, in order to form a mental model of a text which includes cohesion, a reader must be able to see the cohesive relationship between a node and its terminal(s). If a match is not effected, the reader will not fulfill the cohesive potential of the cohesive element. There are several cases in which this phenomenon may occur.

Exophoric nodes. Ordinarily, if *all* readers were to perceive the relationship represented by a particular cohesive tie, both members of such a pair would have to be present in the physical text because this is the only input assured to be common to all readers. That is, in Halliday and Hasan's terms, most tie members will be *endophoric*, or intratextual, but this is not always the case. Sometimes there is no endophoric node available. In such a case, readers must rely on inferring an extratextual, or *exophoric*, node for interpretation.[29]

It may seem counterintuitive to say that a node can be outside the text, but this is not so anomalous in the light of what Hrushovski (1982) calls the "First Sentence Fallacy." He says that there is no such thing as a first sentence, that sentences can only occur in the particular milieu of text users. This suggests that readers should be able to retrieve even extratextual nodes from prior knowledge, and indeed they may be able to infer nonexplicit nodes by carrying out "bridging inferences" (Clark, 1975). In the bridging process, where an "inferential gap" (Kirsner & Thompson, 1976) occurs, the mind

---

[28] The fact that a writer fails to provide an appropriate node in a physical text may be deliberate in some cases where the writer may well believe that the reader will be able to "fill in the blank." In other cases, it may be sloppiness or a deliberate stylistic strategy (Stoddard, 1983). In any case, the reader cannot be expected to secondguess the intention of the writer, but only, where necessary and possible, to make an inference which is reasonable.

[29] Another possibility is that a cohesive element is *homophoric* which Halliday and Hasan (1976) and Gutwinski (1976) consider to be the generic or unique case as in *the voter* and *the moon* respectively. Whether these are genuinely self-referencing is questionable (as suggested in Note 14, Chapter 3).

interprets a cohesive element in the text by finding an extratextual node stored in a frame from past experience or knowledge. A classic case is that of a definite noun phrase or a pronoun at the beginning of a short story with no preceding explicit node possible in the physical text at that point. In this case, the node must be either cataphoric or inferred from outside the written text.

Ambiguous nodes. In some cases, there may be more than one logical, possible node for a given cohesive element in a text, in which case, a reader may see the resulting ambiguity but not be able to decide between (or among) the choices. As Webber (1980, p. 142) points out, "[C]hoosing between possible antecedents [nodes] may demand very sophisticated syntactic, semantic, pragmatic, inferential, and evaluative abilities on the reader's part." If so, some readers may not judge the text cohesive at that point because of the unresolved ambiguity. On the other hand, not all readers will find more than one node, in which case, ambiguity does not arise.

Faulty processing. In still other cases, a written text may have an appropriate node, but some readers may miss it due to sloppy or hasty reading.

Unfulfilled cohesion. Finally, if a reader is not able to find an appropriate intratextual node (either anaphorically or cataphorically), he/she must infer a reasonable extratextual, nonexplicit node. If that does not occur, then, for that person, processing of a particular cohesive element results in *unfulfilled cohesion* which is discussed further in Chapter 3.

Rochester (1976, p. 339) asks a pertinent question for which there is as yet no answer:

> What is not clear, and what has not been studied is the extent to which this failure affects the [reader]. How much unclear noun phrase reference does it take to make discourse incoherent for the [reader]?

Rumelhart (1977, p. 160) claims that in the case of unfulfilled cohesion "a failure in communication results." Whether—or to what extent—this is true is not clear yet. Rumelhart continues, "[V]ery little has been said until we can specify the processes involved in actually *computing* the referent."

Given the complexities attendant to defining cohesion, it is obvious that the complexities of reader processing will not be easily understood. Nevertheless, the nature of cohesion, depending as it does on syntactic signals, allows us to study it with some degree of systematicity.

RESEARCH HYPOTHESES

It is possible to find evidence for a subject's construction of such cohesion—or lack of it—by discovering the cohesion connections made in the process of reading. From this evidence we can show how the patterns of cohesion are created and how they contribute to the texture of texts. This is the aim of the research undertaken here.

Three hypotheses guided the research to analyze the empirical evidence of cohesion and a reader's perception of it in 35 published texts representing 5 text-types. The first hypothesis which deals with frequency of occurrence is stated as follows:

I. The potential for cohesion is a component of all texts, and therefore, will be found with some regularity in all written texts.

Even though the hypothesis is confined to only one text component, there are many types of cohesion to be studied and there are many complexities in doing so. Because of these, the study was limited to three types of cohesion which are discussed in detail in Chapter 3.

Calculating the number of occurrences of cohesive potential suggests the pervasiveness of cohesion in texts, but does not differentiate between texts or between text-types. The second hypothesis, which addresses this issue, is stated as follows:

II. The relative cohesiveness of a text depends on the number of cohesive ties generated by the reader and on the distance between the nodes and their associated cohesive elements.

Neither the frequency of occurrence nor the relative cohesiveness shows how cohesion contributes to texture. Texture is more than the pattern of one type of cohesion in a single text; it is made up of all the various text patterns and their interaction. This interaction, as shown in the patterns of cohesion, forms the basis for the third hypothesis:

III. Patterns of cohesion shown graphically illustrate the rudiments of texture in texts.

"Networks of cohesion" (Halliday & Hasan, 1976) suggest a visual metaphor. Such a graphic description of cohesion patterns can, in fact, be abstracted from a written text by converting the locations of cohesion networks to a "map." Overlaying the maps of three types of cohesive elements results in a rudimentary textural image which suggests that the composite texture of a text emerges from the overlaying of all the various patterns of all text-creating mechanisms. Such an overlay, of course, is not a physical entity but rather a function of the mind's perception.

The three hypotheses, then, take into account one aspect of the synergism of texts resulting from reader processing. If we were to take Hrushovski, Minsky, and Schmidt (p. 3) seriously and begin to analyze the problem space "text" adequately, we would find it an impossible chore at this stage of our technology. However, by limiting such a study to cohesion, an analysis is not impossible and the exploration results add to our understanding of texts.

Textual cohesion is a complex phenomenon, and each type of cohesion displays its own confounding characteristics. The peculiarities of each of the three types tested, namely, definite articles, pronouns, and agent displacements, are considered in Chapter 3. In addition, the method of analysis used to carry out the research is explained.

3
Analyzing Patterns of Cohesion

Designing a research package for an analysis of patterns of cohesion is complicated by the immensity of the potential. The number of types of cohesion, the number of written texts available for analysis, the number of possible readers, and the number of cohesive ties each reader may find in each text is very large. A subsequent analysis of the resulting mass of data—even with the help of modern computers—is daunting. Therefore, the necessity for limiting the scope of research is obvious.

The narrowing can be done in any one or all of several ways. One is the selection of the number and types of cohesion to be analyzed. A second is the selection of the corpus: (a) determining the number and types of written texts to be included, and (b) determining the length of segments and choosing particular segments. A third is the number and qualifications of reader-subjects. Finally, an appropriate and adequate computer program must be written. This chapter discusses the formulation of the research method adopted for this study.

SELECTION OF COHESION TYPES FOR ANALYSIS

Two criteria guided the choice of the cohesive types to be examined. The first criterion, based on the first and second hypotheses (Chapter 2), is the relative number of occurrences of cohesive ties anticipated. That is, those that might be expected to occur most frequently might also be expected to exhibit the most fruitful network patterns. A second criterion, based on the second hypothesis, is the expected relative distances spanned by cohesive ties. That is, types of cohesion which are global in nature (those which cross sentence and paragraph boundaries) might be expected to exhibit the most common patterns. The cohesion types chosen, all of which exhibit this potential, are: (a) pronouns,[1] which Halliday and Hasan[2] categorize under "reference"

---

[1] The personal pronouns analyzed are those which Halliday and Hasan (1976) classify under "reference" with the addition of the "self" pronominals. Because the mind must follow the same cohesion processing for the "self" set as for other pronouns, there is good reason to include them.

32

(1976, p. 333); (b) definite articles which they also categorize under "reference" (1976, p. 333); and (c) agent displacements. This last category does not coincide exactly with any of Halliday and Hasan's categories.

Each of these types has some unique characteristics, but they have common characteristics as well. One of these is common to pronouns and definite articles which are often associated together because, in some sense, they are both "definite." In fact, Postal (1966, p. 179) claims that pronouns are "really articles, in fact types of definite articles." Another common characteristic is the potential for the ellipsis of the node in all three. Yet another is the necessity for a reader to retrieve an appropriate node. While some[3] have thought of retrieval in terms of finding "referents" for their respective "references" and it would be tempting to use this terminology, these terms have been used in so many senses they have lost their precision. For instance, they are sometimes used in a philosophical sense to indicate a relationship between a textual entity and some object in the "real" world or some idea in a person's mind[4] while others use it to mean only an intratextual relationship, and so on. In any case, I avoid the use of the term "referent," preferring "node" as being more descriptive and more precise in talking about cohesion.

A fourth attribute in common is the fact of a semantic relationship between each cohesive element and its node. The nature of this relationship, however, is unique for each type of cohesion. This will become more evident as each type is discussed in more detail in this chapter, but in general, the semantic connections can be characterized as follows: Between pronouns and their nodes, the relationship is one of identity;[5] between definite article phrases and their nodes, several relationships are possible, for example, identity, part/whole, and hierarchy;[6] between passive verbs, *-ed* verbals and *-ing* verbals, and their nodes, the relationship is one of verb and agent.

---

[2] Halliday and Hasan (1976) classify cohesion types into two major categories: grammatical and lexical. Since lexical cohesion, as they have defined it, is not mutually exclusive from other types of cohesion, I did not entertain its inclusion in this study even though lexical cohesion can operate globally.

[3] The following are some of those who do: DoBois (1980), Rochester and Martin (1977), Webber (1980,1981), Rumelhart (1977), Norman and Rumelhart (1975), Hawkins (1978), de Beaugrande (1980).

[4] Seldom is an actual object which is mentioned in a particular written text present during the reading of a text (as, for instance, the cave described in Hemingway's *For Whom the Bell Tolls*). There may, of course, be exceptions such as reading about the Statue of Liberty in a tour guide book while standing at her feet.

[5] A common exception to this is that of plural pronouns where the inclusiveness of the pronoun is unclear, but it may also happen in the case where a plural subject such as *the Gardners* is the antecedent of *she* which in the context clearly means the female partner of the couple.

[6] The typologies of Chafe (1976, pp. 39–40), Clark and Marshall (1981, p. 22), de Beaugrande (1980, p. 138), and Hawkins (1978, p. 106f) do not adequately address these relationships.

The remainder of this chapter discusses each selected cohesion type and describes the method formulated to carry out the research. Definite articles which are perhaps the most complex of the three types are examined first, followed by pronouns, and finally agent displacements.

Definite Articles

The definite article, which is the syntactic indicator of one type of cohesive element, is only part of a larger syntactic structure, the definite noun phrase. In actuality, it is the noun to which the definite article is attached which has the cohesive and semantic relationship with its node. However, since the definite article is the syntactic marking of the cohesive element and since not all noun phrases contain a definite article, it is more convenient to talk about the "definite article" though it is understood that it is only part of a definite noun phrase. I do so here with the understanding that it is simply a convenience.[7] It should be noted also that some noun phrases are definite in meaning without being marked by definite articles. These were not included in this study but are discussed below.

To understand how the definite article operates as a cohesive element, it will be helpful to consider a passage such as the beginning of the first paragraph of Mari Sandoz's biography, *Old Jules,* which is given in (1).[8] (See Appendix A.)

> (1) The border towns of Rock and Cherry counties were shaking off the dullness of winter. Galloping hoofs, the boom of the forty-four, and the measured beat of the spike-maul awakened the narrow single streets running between the tents and shacks. Sky pilots plodded from town to town, preaching a scorching and violent hell. But west of there the monotonous yellow sandhills unobtrusively soaked up the soggy patches of April snow.

It is probable that readers in general will, on encountering a definite noun phrase, begin a search (however unconsciously) for the most appropriate cohesive node. We might envision the following scenario. On reading the first words of the passage above, readers seeing the phrase *the border towns* might wonder how Sandoz intended the cohesive tie to be interpreted,[9]

---

[7] In marking the texts for analysis, however, I marked the noun rather than the definite article because the noun provides more information.

[8] This example is admittedly brief in terms of my general notion that we need to look at longer stretches of text, but it is sufficient for this illustration.

[9] Even if we consult a living author, he/she may not be able to recollect intent at a particular point. In reading written texts, we simply do not have access to a writer's intention; we are essentially dependent on resources other than the writer for interpretation. This is true in spite of the fact that linguists continue to speak as if it were possible to discern *intent* in all forms of

because there is no preceding node available. Thus, *the towns* cannot be anaphoric. Even so, readers probably assume that the writer has not used *the* preceding *towns* in a frivolous way (Grice's Cooperative Principle, 1975). They may trust that Hrushovski's First Sentence fallacy (1982) is correct. If they accept that every first sentence has some relation to knowledge-frames already operational in their minds, they will try to cooperate with the writer. This means they will expect that either (a) the cohesive element with the definite article syntactic signal, *the towns,* will be identified cataphorically within the text, or (b) a reasonable frame-node can be inferred extratextually. If they decide that the definite noun phrase is specified by *Rock and Cherry counties,* they need not search further. If not, they will need to look for some identifying frame-node from previous knowledge, or create a new frame node, or give up the search and acknowledge an unfulfilled cohesive element. Because different strategies are possible, different readers may adopt different conclusions in this case, resulting in differences of interpretation in spite of the fact that we use the term "definite" article.

If readers use a trial-and-error strategy such as I have described, it would be very inefficient and therefore unlikely to reflect actual processing.[10] Gentner's Connectivity Hypothesis (1981) suggests that we probably seek an appropriate frame which has the greatest number of semantic ties to the cohesive element. This is probably more efficient searching than random trials, but the factor of frequency of use may also enter in.

Sanford and Garrod (1980) report experiments conducted to determine the relative recall speed for items frequently used as opposed to those less often used (e.g., "vehicle" is low dominance while "car" is high dominance.) The results show consistently that high-dominance items are more accessible (i.e., recalled with greater speed) than low-dominance items. Sanford and Garrod (1980, p. 470) say:

> The idea of the scenario [frame] is that noun phrases and the actions in which they are involved can serve to call up from memory complex modular information structures that are based upon the reader's experience of related (or identical) situations . . .

This suggests that, though our minds may trigger several possible, suitable frames, depending on the context, it is probably true that those with the higher dominance (higher frequency of use) are most likely to be tested first, thus increasing the processing efficiency. Some readers, having tested all the

---

communication. For instance, Webber (1980, p. 142) says: If a reader cannot handle an anaphoric expression [i.e., a pro-form or a definite noun phrase] *as the writer intended,* there is no way that he or she can correctly update his or her discourse model in response to it" [emphasis added].

[10] de Beaugrande (1980) has an interesting and valuable perspective on the notion of text efficiency.

possibilities perceived for *the towns,* might conclude that the cataphoric node *Rock and Cherry counties* is the most logical expression to fulfill the cohesive tie, and being content with the choice, push on. Whether the writer intended this specification is unknowable. Other readers may or may not come to the same conclusion. Rochester and Martin (1977, p. 261) suggest that "perhaps the problem of using a strategy and the hierarchy of testing those strategies depends on the listener's [reader's] own placement of referents," but to the best of my knowledge, this is untested.

In any case, readers face the same processing dilemma with the ensuing definite noun phrases *the forty-four* and *the spike-maul* whose interpretation depends heavily on historical-cultural knowledge. In contrast, *the streets, the tents,* and *the shacks* are likely to be easily associated with *the towns*. But then the question arises as to whether these features are "definite" by virtue of their being specified by another definite noun phrase *the towns,* or by virtue of being terminals of the same node to which *the towns* is tied. This uncertainty about the node to which a definite noun phrase terminal is attached creates a kind of ambiguity which allows a variation in interpretation among readers.[11] The remaining definite noun phrases in the passage seem less problematical.

The point of this discussion of Sandoz' initial paragraph is that the term "definite" is far too ill-defined to assume that we can agree as to its meaning. DuBois (1980, p. 208) very perceptively suggests that:

> Because of the great confusion which has existed in the past over what definiteness is, and because it is not in fact possible to specify a single function of the definite article which will apply in all areas of English grammar, it is perhaps best to divorce the question of semantic/pragmatic function from the question of formal marking. The word *definite* may serve a useful purpose in referring to a formal class of reference items . . .

Unfortunately, as Chafe (1976, p. 39) says, "we are stuck with the traditional label." If we continue to use it, we must be very clear about certain questions: (a) What do we mean when we say that a certain phrase is "definite"? (b) To whom is it definite? (c) By virtue of what standard do we judge its definiteness? In answer to the first question, de Beaugrande (1980, p. 133) defines definiteness as "the extent to which the text-world entity for an expression at a given point is assumed to be identifiable and recoverable, as opposed to being introduced just then." This indicates that the "text-world entity" (the node) should be old information retrievable from previous text, but by deleting the agents for *assumed to be identifiable and recoverable* and *being intro-*

---

[11] There seems to be virtually no discussion of this aspect of definiteness except perhaps for Clark's (1975) discussion of bridging.

duced, de Beaugrande leaves the question of agency of these verbals unclear. If he means that the writer assumes that readers can identify and recover the node from previous text, then if the writer is wrong (i.e., readers cannot or do not), it means that only the writer perceives the relationship between the node and the cohesive element ("an expression"). If he means that readers assume that they should be able to identify and recover the "text-world entity," then does a failure to do so on their part mean that the "expression" is "indefinite"? In any case, de Beaugrande assumes that definiteness can only be intratextual. He does not account for the instances where readers must infer extratextual nodes from their knowledge frames to match cohesive elements in the physical text if cohesion is to exist at all.

In contrast, Chafe (1976, p. 39) suggests that if a writer thinks readers can identify particular nodes, he/she "will give this item the status of definite . . . [but] *identifiable* would be a better term than definite." This explanation is given from the writer's point of view, but even if the writer regards an expression to be "definite and thus identifiable by a reader," in fact, it may not be. (This very case is discussed below.) From the readers' point of view, the writer's evaluation of an expression as "definite and identifiable" is irrelevant; readers have only the syntactic signals in a physical text, not the writer's intent. We can only conclude that whatever degree of definiteness is available for analysis lies in the minds of readers. Hawkins (1978, p. 97) confirms this saying that one of the appropriateness conditions of definite reference (cohesion) must be "hearer [reader] orientation."[12]

Another aspect of definiteness which needs clarification is that, as DuBois suggests above, definiteness, a semantic notion, is not indicated syntactically by the definite article alone; some personal pronouns, demonstratives, some substitutives, proper names, and other noun phrases without any article attached may be said by readers to be "definite." Conversely, just as definiteness is not always signaled by definite articles, so the definite article does not always express definiteness. In the case of the excerpt in (a), Sandoz herself may have had an appropriate frame to which to attach *the forty-four* and *the spike-maul* by virtue of her study of the history of the period, and thus she may have labeled them "definite" in her mind. But, without an intratextual node, readers who do not have such a frame will find it difficult to think of these expressions as "definite." In fact, for readers who don't have appropriate frames (for whatever reason), these expressions are just as indefinite as *sky pilots* which is not preceded by the definite article. Indeed, definiteness and the definite article do not necessarily coincide.

If interpretation of definite articles does not always imply definiteness,

---

[12] In spite of this, Hawkins (1978 p. 152) continues to believe with the philosophers that a referent (node) must be "an identifiable object" and that the hearer has access to the writer's intention.

then why are definite article noun phrases included in this study while other "definite" noun phrases are excluded? Two reasons justify the category, I believe. One is that definite article *the* is a "pure" syntactic marking. That is, it stands alone, never changes form, and is easily identified.

The second reason is more complicated. It is based on the premise that the definiteness of definite article noun phrases can be described as either definite or not definite. A writer may, in fact, believe an expression to be definite, or specified, but until readers agree, we cannot say that it is. To make a judgment of definiteness, readers must find an appropriate frame node from the physical text or from frames stored in their minds. Finding a frame-node allows a noun phrase to be "interpreted" as definite:[13] that is, frame-nodes delimit noun phrases. Where a logical, explicit node exists in the physical text, there is no problem. In the case where there is no available node in the physical text, the definite noun phrase may be frame-specified if a reader is able to find a satisfying, logical extratextual frame-node either from memory or by creating one. Such frames are subject to variation from reader to reader, but nonetheless, for each reader who succeeds in supplying a suitable frame, definiteness exists. In this sense, and this sense only, can we continue to use the term "definite" noun phrase with precision.

On the other hand, if a reader does not have or cannot create an appropriate frame, it is hard to see how the noun phrase can be said to be definite. Instances of definite article noun phrases which are not so specified by either an explicit or an inferred node cannot be said to be "definite." Instead, such cases must be classified as unfulfilled cohesion (discussed in Chapter 2).[14] As the data and discussion in Chapter 4 demonstrate, all the texts analyzed in this study contain such noninterpretable instances. This means that writers apparently do not intend to make all their ideas explicit[15] and it further confirms the fallacy of the Conduit Metaphor (Chapter 1).

---

[13] This is different than the *writer's believing* it to be interpretable by the reader.

[14] It is quite possible that in this situation readers create a new frame using the definite noun phrase itself as the frame node. If so, the definite article in this case does not function in the same manner as the definite article which is a true signal to find a specifying node. It may be that such situations fit what Gutwinski (1976) calls "homophoric" which implies that the definite noun phrase is self-specifying (e.g., *the sun*). Such cases could be classified as being different from those definite noun phrases which rely on frame nodes for interpretation. However, I believe that a thorough study of such cases will reveal that they might be better classed as having extratextual nodes. For instance, we now know that *the moon* we've talked about for centuries is not the only one, yet it may take many more years and much more interstellar travel to have this now-outmoded usage reflected in our language.

[15] An alternative view of the existence of nonavailable nodes is provided by duBois who looks at the definite article from an historical point of view. Although articles were seldom used in earlier periods of English, DuBois says that where they were used a specific referent was usually mentioned. Now we use them ubiquitously where there is no other determiner so that articles have lost a part of their original function. "The result is that the so-called definite article in many cases no longer marks definiteness, even if one equates definiteness with identifiability" (1980 p. 207).

Even where a definite noun phrase is interpretable and specified there is leeway for different readers to vary in their interpretation of definite noun phrases depending on their perception of the relationship between the frame-node and the noun phrase (discussed earlier in this chapter). Although it is not the purpose of this study to construct a typology of the various relationships between the noun phrases in these passages and their nodes, understanding the variations among them is useful in explaining the complexities involved in processing cohesion. Some examples will illustrate the problem. (See Appendix A.)

> (2) Maycomb was an old town . . . In rainy weather the streets turned to red slop; grass grew on the side-walks, the courthouse sagged in the square . . . Bony mules hitched to Hoover carts flicked flies in the sweltering shade of the live oaks on the square. (Lee, *To Kill a Mockinobird*)
>
> (3) . . . They asked each student what college he was in—that is, whether Arts, Engineering, Commerce, or Agriculture . . . Haskins didn't seem cut out for journalism . . . but the editor of the college-paper assigned him to the cow barns, the sheep house, the horse pavilion, and the animal husbandry department generally. (Thurber, "University Days")

Maycomb is the obvious frame in the passage from Lee's book, but from there, the particular semantic relationships evidenced between the terminals and their frame nodes are open to interpretation. For instance, the relationship between the node *Maycomb* and those terminals that are part of the built environment (*the streets, the sidewalks, the courthouse*) is distinct from those that are not (*the oaks*). Not all the node-cohesive element relationships are so clear-cut though. Depending on a reader's point of view, *the square* may be interpreted as a geographic entity (i.e., a part of the earth-landscape), or it may be interpreted as altered by the town's inhabitants and thus a human-made feature. Also problematical is the possibility of hierarchical subframing. In this passage, *the shade* has a direct relationship to the noun phrase *the oaks* which in turn has a direct relationship to *the square* which is specified by the town of *Maycomb*. Is each in turn a subframe, or is each a terminal associated directly with the frame node *Maycomb*? One aspect to consider in defining all these relationships is the perception of *Maycomb* itself as a political subdivision, a geographic entity, a human social community, and people's mental perceptions of it. Certainly the representation of knowledge in our minds is a crucial issue in language use. Another example will confirm this.

The relationships between definite noun phrases and possible nodes in the Thurber excerpt (3) are equally complex. Whether journalism is a subframe of the university-frame will determine whether *the college paper* is specified by a journalism-frame or the university-frame. Readers may also vary in their interpretation of *the college paper* as a terminal of one or the other. Then the question arises as to whether *the editor*, being the producer of *the college paper* is tied to it or to *journalism.* The relationship between *the college of agriculture* and various animal shelters is different than that between *the college of agriculture* and *the animal husbandry department,* the former being the location of the material for study and the latter being an administrative unit of the college. How readers resolve these questions must certainly relate to their reading strategies, a challenging area of study.

I have yet to discuss the question of the standards by which we judge "definiteness" which I raised earlier. As this discussion has shown, there seem to be degrees of definiteness. (For instance, we seem to sense that some definite noun phrases are more clearly specified than others though this was not mentioned by Lakoff, 1976.) In other words, how definite does an expression have to be in the minds of readers before they classify it as definite? This potential for variability is related to Gentner's Connectivity Hypothesis (1981). It is also related to the question of how hard readers will work to find a suitable node, to fulfill what seems like it *ought* to be definite. We could, as Clark (1975) points out, build any number of inferential bridges to fulfill definite article cohesion, but do we do it? And do we do it all the time? And do we do it for all texts?[16] Webber (1980, p. 151) suggests that:

> [T]he more contingent an inference becomes, the more that judgments on the consequent existence of an antecedent or referent [node] will vary from person to person . . . [P]eople might vary as to the amount of effort they will expend inferring an antecedent or referent or as to whether they will expend any effort at all!

Until we test how willing and how persistent readers are in establishing cohesive ties from definite articles and what their perceptions of relative definiteness are, we probably will not be able to find a satisfactory answer to the question of the standards readers use to judge definiteness. Nevertheless, because most nodes for syntactically marked definite noun phrases can be identified, it is logical that they be included in a study of cohesion patterns.

In summary, the definite article cohesive element provides information to the reader about how the noun phrase to which it is attached can be integrated into the text being processed. This integration depends on the degree of definiteness perceived, the level of dominance of the definite noun phrase, and the ability of the reader to find a suitable frame-node and interpret the semantic relationship adhering between the lexical items at the ends of the cohesive tie.

Pronouns

To some extent this same integrative process applies to pronoun cohesive elements as well. Pronouns operate like definite articles in some ways. On the

---

[16] If I as reader-subject, deliberately looking for nodes, gave up occasionally, what would the average reader (who does not have a vested interest) do?

one hand, pronouns may express a certain kind of reader-identified/node-specified definiteness. On the other, not all nodes for pronouns are retrievable intratextually, nor are they always easily inferred. Where the node is clear, there should be no variation among readers in interpreting them, but several kinds of personal pronouns by their very nature are ambiguous unless specifically defined. Intuitively we might think that the use of pronouns is less complex than the use of definite articles because theoretically there is a single semantic relationship of identity between pronouns and their nodes. However, an analysis of pronouns as cohesive elements shows that they are not simple. A discussion of first-, second-, and third-person pronouns will point out the possible inconsistencies.[17]

Even though the third person singular personal pronouns are marked by gender (or lack of it) and number, their nodes are not always easily identified. The singular form *it* is problematic because of its multipurpose nature. Those instances where *it* is not a personal pronoun (as in "dummy" subjects and clausal substitutions) were excluded from the study. In the case of the generic *he,* the very genericness of the male pronoun is called into question by studies which show that both males and females interpret the male pronoun as applying to males only.[18] Certainly readers with different world views are likely to interpret the frame node of the so-called generic *he* differently. The third form of the third person singular pronoun, *she,* seldom exhibits ambiguity. This is not true of the plural form, however. As Halliday and Hasan (1976) and de Beaugrande (1980) point out, *they* is a "vague agent" which is sometimes ambiguous as to the specific number and identity of persons or things to be identified as node, but the results of this study show that this problem is miniscule.

The first and second person pronouns can also be problematic. De Beaugrande (1980, p. 152) claims that "first and second person pronouns are inherently exophoric, and their use presupposes the mutual identifiability of the communicative participants, though more directly for speaking than for writing." This claim indicates that, when writers write, they do so on the assumption that readers will be able to identify the frame nodes for the first and second person pronouns from the situational context. We might make allowances for amateur writers who do not write "clearly," but we might expect that professional writers would not leave ambiguous loose ends. Such is not the case, however.

It is true that in some kinds of writing. *you* may be used to mean the readers, individually or as a set. But in other cases the frame to which the

---

[17] The discussion that follows applies to all morphological forms of each pronoun and not just the subjective form as used here.

[18] Even though language conservatives would have us believe that *he* is applicable to all persons (generic), recent studies, suggest otherwise (e.g., Eberhart, 1976; Kidd, 1971; Mackay, 1983; Mackay & Fulkerson, 1979; Martyna, 1978).

second-person pronoun is tied is less clear. Here the relationship between written and spoken texts is important. In casual conversation, we often slip into using *you*, and if there is a question, the listener can ask the speaker for a clarification, but readers cannot ask writers for an explanation. This means that readers, on encountering the potentially ambiguous *you* must infer what is meant. For instance, the second-person pronouns in the following passage from Bradbury's "August 2002" are not unambiguous. (See Appendix A.) Here the old man says to Tomas:

> (4) I came to Mars to retire and I wanted to retire in a place where everything is different. An old man needs to have things different. Young people don't want to talk to him, or other old people bore the hell out of him. So I thought the best thing for me is a place so different that all you got to do is open your eyes and you're entertained.

Certainly the old man doesn't mean the reader, but does he mean Tomas? Or only old people? Or just himself? We don't know. Whether it *matters* or not that we don't know relates to how much readers accept on faith.

The first-person pronouns present another kind of problem. As de Beaugrande points out, a written text is assumed by the reader to have a writer—an exophoric *I*. But such a text may have an intratextual narrator *I* as well. This may cause initial confusion for some readers, but if the identify of the *I* is made clear in the context, there should be little confusion. In still other cases, such as conversations in stories, the *I* which belongs to a node-participant in the intratextual conversation should be clear enough as in the excerpt in (4).

The first person plural *we* is ambiguous in ways similar to *you, they,* and the generic *he*. This is true in spite of the fact that de Beaugrande (1980, p. 152) dismisses *we* as "institutionalized exophoric reference" saying: "A partly non-determinate 'we' lets speaker include self and *any number of prototypical others*" (emphasis added). In so doing, de Beaugrande imputes the best of motives to every writer.[19] Where *we* clearly means multiple authorship, the reader should have no problem, but it is common practice in scholarly treatises (for whatever reason) to use *we* when there is only one author, even as I have done here. In this situation and others such as in propaganda, the use of *we* (unless the writer gives prior specification to those persons who are to be included in the pronoun) also allows an author to claim, by default, greater acceptability of his/her hypotheses than is warranted. The following excerpt from one of the texts analyzed in this study is but one example of the use of the so-called "editorial *we*" which demonstrates the possibility of affecting the readers' perceptions of the topic under discussion. The brevity of this

---

[19] As Stanley (1978) points out, a writer's motives may not always be pure.

excerpt in itself, of course, may distort a valid analysis, but it does illustrate the problem of an "institutionalized exophoric reference." (See Appendix A.)

> (5) What we need is a technology of behavior. We could solve our problems quickly enough if we could adjust the growth of the world's population as precisely as we adjust the course of a spaceship . . . (Skinner, *Beyond Freedom and Dignity*)

Is every instance of *we* in this passage constituted of the same persons? Who are the "prototypical others" of whom de Beaugrande speaks? And is it important who they are? (And who are included in the *we* in this book *you* are reading.) It is obvious that, although pronouns are not unlike definite articles as cohesive elements, they are not without their own peculiarities to be reckoned with in determining how cohesive they may be in certain situations. The question is how such problems affect a reader's perception of cohesion.

Agent Displacements

Unlike the semantic relationships between pronoun cohesive elements and definite article cohesive elements and their nodes, the cohesive element-node relationship for cases of agent displacement involves an agent and a verb or verbal. Freeman (1979, p. 147) points out that "verbs and words derived from verbs have more obligations than other words do." One of these obligations is that, to be fully interpretable by the reader, verbs and verbals in English require agents (whether explicit or implicit).[20] The nodes in this type of cohesion are the agents and the cohesive elements are the associated passive verbs and *-ing* and *-ed* verbals.[21]

In English it is possible to "displace" agents in certain circumstances.[22] Even though they are displaced, if the agent-nodes are intratextual, they should be readily accessed by the reader; if they are not, they will, like other nonexplicit nodes, require the reader to infer or create an agent.[23] Examples

---

[20] I use "agent" here as opposed to "subject" because the "agent" (which is a semantic notion) is not the syntactic subject of a passive verb although the concepts coincide for other types of verbs.

[21] It may seem counterintuitive to identify the agent as the node in agent displacement, rather than the passive verbs or the *-ed* and *-ing* verbals. However, the cohesive element, as defined in Chapter 2, is marked by a syntactic signal indicating the need for another expression, the node, to complete its interpretation. In the case of agent displacement, the passive verb and *-ed* and *-ing* verbals are so marked.

[22] This type of cohesion is not unlike ellipsis involving participles. Thompson (1983) defines a category she calls "detached participles." While detached participles are involved in agent displacement, her category cannot deal with the agent-predicate relationship which adheres for all verbs and verbals.

[23] Stanley and Wolfe (1977) discuss the problem of the agent-truncated passive very cogently

from data analyzed in this study illustrate four types of possible agent displacements. (See Appendix A.)

> (6) Often he worked alone in the timbers, all day long with only the sound of his own ax, or his own voice speaking to himself, or the crackling and swaying of branches in the wind . . .(Sandburg, *Lincoln: the Prairie Years*)
>
> (7) It was about three when we rode into Bridger's Wells, past the boarded-up church on the right, with its white paint half-cracked off, and the houses back under the cottonwoods, or between rows of flickering poplars . . . (Clark, *The Ox-Bow Incident*).
>
> (8) Similar situations are legion, involving unexpectedness, interest, and other emotional reactions on the part of the speaker to what he is talking about. Thus, while two speakers may be talking about the same thing or real-world situation, their descriptions may end up sounding utterly unrelated. The following well-known paradigm will be illustrative. (Lakoff, *Language and Woman's Place*)
>
> (9) Something about Miss Minnie Cooper and a Negro. Attacked, insulted, frightened: none of them, gathered in the barber shop on that Saturday evening where the ceiling fan stirred, without freshening it, the vitiated air, sending back upon them, in recurrent surges of stale pomade and lotion, their own stale breath and odors, knew exactly what had happened. (Faulkner, "Dry September")
>
> (10) In the year 1357 a piece of linen cloth about 14 feet long and bearing the dorsal and ventral images of a man's body was exhibited in a collegiate church belonging to the de Charny family in Lirey, France. It was said to be the burial shroud of Jesus, the imprint being that of his body. (Thomsen, "The Shroud of Turin: A Shroud of Unknowing")

The categories of agent displacement common in written texts of all types are listed below with examples from the data above:

1. the passive verb without an immediately present agent, as in (10): *body was exhibited* (by whom?), *it was said* (by whom?)
2. the passive verbal (i.e., auxiliary deleted) without an immediately present agent, as in (7): *the boarded-up church* (boarded up by whom?), *the half-cracked off paint* (cracked by what?)
3. the *-ing* verbal (i.e., auxiliary deleted) with immediate agent, as in (6) and (10): *voice speaking* and *church belonging*
4. the *-ing* verbal with agent moved to a post position or displaced elsewhere in the text or located outside the text, as in (7), (8), and (9): *flickering poplars, situations . . . involving* and *fan . . . sending*

---

and cite numerous examples.

It might be argued that case 3, where the agent is immediate, is not truly a case of agent displacement. However, I believe that, because it involves auxiliary deletion and because the agent can sometimes be moved to a position immmediately following the verbal or elsewhere, it fits the category of agent displacement. It might also be argued that infinitives as verbals should have been included in the study, and indeed, there is good reason for doing so. However, they were excluded because of the added complexities of their syntactic structure.

Agent displacement has the effect of forcing cooperative readers to attempt to identify the agent for the passive verb and *-ed* and *-ing* verbals in order to construct mental models of the writer's text. That is, cohesion in this case depends on the reader's being able to make such cohesive ties whether the agent-node is immediately present or not.

These three types of cohesion lend themselves well to analysis by computer. They are relatively discrete, they are numerous, and they are relatively easy to define. Furthermore, they are essential components of texture in text. The next sections discuss the factors that must be taken into consideration in doing text analysis in general and in devising a specific method which can be used to carry out the computer analysis.

SELECTION OF A CORPUS

If we assume that there are standards which define a text, we must also assume that competent readers accept them as standards for all written texts.[24] Linguistic expressions that are found to deviate from accepted standards will be judged in one of two ways; (a) Such deviations may be considered true aberrations, or (b) they may call into question the standards themselves, revealing the need for revision. A consistent exception may demonstrate that different standards exist for different types of texts (as suggested by Schmidt, 1977) and require us to reclassify the data and revise the standards. However, until we know more about what kinds of componential regularities do exist in texts in general and in the several genres, we cannot determine standards. As Schmidt and others have suggested, we will need to have evidence from many texts.

This raises the question of an appropriate and sufficient database for discourse analysis of this kind. This question is especially critical in the study of written texts. as Kroeber (1966, p. 58) points out:

> If one assumes he understands the essential mysteries of language and can display them in brief, invented sentences, one is unlikely to exploit the oppor-

---

[24] We do not, of course, have a norm by which to judge who is a "competent" reader, but we know that there is no such person as the "ideal" reader that Fillmore (1982) discusses.

tunities provided by fine literature to discover the fullest achievement and richest potentialities of the language.

In spite of Kroeber's statement, there seems to be very little criticism of the data used by linguists as the basis for testing their discourse theories. I believe this is an unfortunate and rather basic oversight. Two faults are common. One is the attempt to explain text phenomena by analyzing a minimal quantity of data (e.g., sequences of two to three sentences). The other is the analysis of data contrived by theoreticians themselves for purposes of illustration.[25] In fact, Kock (1973), Minsky (1975), and Schmidt (1977) agree with Hrushovski (1982, p. 159) that we need to "reverse the order of investigation: [to] use literary texts for the observation of language phenomena and the construction of a more adequate theory."

By using self-authored passages as databases, discourse linguists risk invalidating the results in one of two ways. For one thing, short, contrived examples (as opposed to published data written for other purposes) may, when put in another context, cast doubt on the researcher's conclusions. That is, since that notion "text" cannot be totally isolated from the processing environment, all contrived examples—if we continue to use such—should be tested in appropriate linguistic environments. Furthermore, examples of passages only two or three sentences long do not allow analysis of many text properties which are global, not local, in nature. In many studies purporting to explain text principles, the examples are researcher-written and too few in number and too short to be adequately tested.[26] There is only one answer to Kroeber's criticism: select substantial amounts of a wide variety of "real" data written for purposes other than the particular study being undertaken.

The possibilities of a database for text studies are many. One might study biographies, and only biographies, over a limited period of time; one might study biographies cross-culturally in the period from 1900–1920; one might look at American political essays in each election year since the Civil War; and so on. For an initial exploration of the text-forming properties of patterns of cohesion, a broad spectrum of written texts is most likely to yield a general view of that aspect of the problem space. However, confounding the study by adding such factors as archaic language, distinctive dialects of English (e.g., Indian English), writer competence, and co-authors unnecessarily increases the variables at this stage. On the other hand, narrowing the corpus too much (an as yet undefined quantity) can also be a problem.

The corpus selected, then, includes only works by 20th-century writers

---

[25] When scholars claim no more for their studies of single sentences or smaller units than is warranted, this criticism does not hold. Nevertheless, using natural language data—even in sentence-length units (as Stanley, 1975, does)—strengthens the results.

[26] Notable exceptions include: Gutwinski (1976) and Ellegard (1978).

published in the United States. It includes one work by each of 35 writers, seven in each of five conventionally accepted text-types: novels, short stories, essays, biographies, and booklength nonfiction prose (the last hereafter referred to as simply "nonfiction").[27]

The choice of passages within texts introduces other considerations. To show globalness, the segments to be analyzed have to be long enough to include several paragraphs. In the shorter works (short stories and essays), a minimum of 1200 words of continuous text beginning with the opening sentence fulfills this stricture. Booklength texts, on the other hand, afford an opportunity not only to check for distance as a factor in cohesion, but also to check for internal consistency (although no formal analysis has been done here). For these, shorter passages—a minimum of 800 words—in each of two passages, constitute the database.

The actual location of a segment within a longer text may affect whether a reader is able to associate a cohesive element with an appropriate node. Globalness should operate within any given segment of text whether such segments initiate the discourse or occur at one of its breakpoints (e.g., the beginning of a chapter, section, or paragraph). However, if a particular node does not occur in the particular passage chosen, but does occur in the physical text preceding the passage to be analyzed, there is a potential for the reader who starts reading midtext to judge the node to be extratextual when, in fact, this is not the case. To minimize this possibility, most segments analyzed begin at a discoursal breakpoint, but never, in any case, in the middle of a sentence or a paragraph.

SELECTION OF A READER-SUBJECT

Most written texts are available to a wide variety of readers who vary considerably in the background, experience, and ability they bring to their reading. Even so, general reading texts, such as biography, fiction, newspapers, and magazines that do not require a technical or specialized vocabulary should be comprehensible to the vast majority of competent readers. We would expect that such readers agree to a large extent in their interpretation of nonesoteric texts and that, consequently, there is minimal variation in their interpretation of cohesive ties. Given this intuitive prediction, I used only one reader-subject, myself.

There are, of course, reasons why using the researcher as reader is less than optimal, but in each case of objection, there are reasons why the option should not be rejected. For one thing, the question of bias could be a confounding problem because of the unavoidable intrusion of the researcher

---

[27] Appendix A contains a list of the published texts analyzed.

into the research process.[28] One could challenge the results of my reading as being affected by my desire as a researcher to have them "come out right." However, with the sheer size of the corpus, it is doubtful that the results could be consciously skewed in one direction or another.

It might also be said that the researcher as subject cannot avoid subjectivity. It is true that any scholar dealing with human phenomena is liable to subjectivity. But it can be argued that researchers are also readers, and all readers, as members of a particular cultural community, necessarily bring particular experiences to the reading of a text. Likewise, writers cannot avoid a conscious and unconscious awareness of the writing strategies of others. In other words, it is nearly impossible for any group of reader-writers to maintain a consistent degree of objectivity, so this should not obviate the method used here.

Someone may argue that a single reader is not necessarily a representative sample of the reading public, except insofar as that person qualifies as a competent reader. Ideally, of course, a wide spectrum of readers should be tested. Certainly if this were a probablistic study rather than a descriptive study more readers would be essential to validate that kind of statistics. Nevertheless, as a first approach to a method of discourse analysis of one type of textural element, the use of a single reader is not without merit.

Furthermore, the number of hours required for each subject to read and mark the cohesive elements and their nodes in a 60,000 word corpus is prohibitive for most subjects. (Even in the computer age it is a forbidding task—a fact which no doubt has kept many scholars from analyzing lengthy passages of texts.) Whether a sufficient number of subjects could have been found to put in an equal number of hours (paid or unpaid) for a study of this scope is doubtful.

In the end, the exploratory nature of this research justifies the use of a single reader who is also the analyst. The results, though limited, are promising and nontrivial. In this case, the opportunity to test the method as suggestive of a direction for future research is important, as are the results.

DESIGNING A COMPUTER PROGRAM

It is obvious, as Ashby points out (1964), that texts are much too complex to assume that we can look at one component at a time in isolation. We need to know how the various text components interact. Nevertheless, even with use of sophisticated computers, we do not yet have the capability to analyze all of the text-forming components at once, let alone their interactions; there are

---

[28] Social scientists have long taken into account the fact that their presence can and does often affect the validity of their study results.

simply too many and their interactions not well understood.[29] Still, we can explore part of the problem space "text" by discovering the most promising way to use the computer to show some interaction and to evaluate whether the questions asked are promising or not.

Although the computer greatly reduces the time needed to analyze texts, it is limited in that it only processes patterns serially by matching previously defined and/or previously marked terms. This has two implications. For one thing, this means that humans must still do a considerable amount of the matching—at best a tedious process and liable to error. For another, it seems highly unlikely, in the light of language-processing research, that the mind is so inefficient as to process pattern-matching serially.

In the past, the computer has been used for a number of linguistic analyses but, by and large, discourse researchers have confined their work to the kinds of analyses which result in lists or counts or concordances.[30] These analyses are useful but limited because they ultimately do not tell us much about how humans produce, process, and interpret texts. Do we know any more about how writers write or readers read, for instance, by learning that Hemingway in *For Whom the Bell Tolls* uses nouns X times more often than Clark does in *The Ox-Bow Incident*? Probably not—until we understand the particular reason why nouns are more useful in one writer's style than in another's. We need an innovative approach to text analysis by computer which will help us explain why we understand texts as we do.

To say that all lists, counts, and concordances have no use would be inaccurate, of course. The problem is that we have not made as effective a use of such results as we could. In the program developed for this study, for example, the descriptive statistics can become input for more sophisticated processing, especially the program which, by showing the interaction between different kinds of cohesion, suggests the formation of texture.

Earlier in this chapter, the functional characteristics of cohesion were established. The kinds of characteristics that the computer can show have to do the frequencies of occurrence of cohesive nodes and elements and their locations. The SNOBOL4 computer language with its string-processing and pattern-matching capability is particularly appropriate for this first phase of analysis.

Three SNOBOL4 programs count and locate elements and nodes and calculate the distances between nodes and their elements. (A portion of the program commands for definite articles is shown in part in Appendix C.) The

---

[29] This is true in spite of the fact that those working in artificial intelligence have made great strides toward programming computers to be "smart." The work of Schank and Abelson 1977, Minsky 1975, John R. Anderson 1976, and others is interesting and shows progress in the field, but the fact remains that computers depend on people for their intelligence—as yet.

[30] Studies such as the following are numerous in the literature: Ellegard (1978), Sedelow and Sedelow (1966), Galloway (1978), Milic (1967), and Kroeber (1967).

basic computer programs for the analysis of each type of cohesion are similar, but are adjusted for the uniqueness of each type.

For input data, the reader marks each node of the written text segment with a pair of delimiters and an identification number. The cohesive elements are marked with a different kind of delimiters and a number matching the associated node. (The two kinds of agent displacements require different kinds of delimiters for both kinds of cohesive elements and their nodes.) An identification number of zero (O) indicates an unfulfilled cohesive element (without an identifiable node). General words (i.e., words not directly involved in cohesive ties) are ignored, except to be counted in the total number of words in the text. An example of pronoun-marking in Sandburg's *Lincoln: The Prairie Years* is shown in Figure 3.1. (See Appendix A.)

This marking method can be used for other types of linguistic analysis and is reasonably simple as long as single words are being marked. An adjustment would have to be devised for some kinds of linguistic data, such as embedded clauses and separable two-word verbs where an object intervenes. In the corpus examined here, the only adjustments necessary are in instances where a hyphen is used to join the parts of a proper name to create a single word for computing (such as *Abe-Lincolns* in Figure 3.1).

Many subjective decisions regarding the marking of the computer input are required. One of these, the decision to arbitrarily name a particular word as a node in the absence of an intratextual, but readily inferrable, extratextual node, is a possibility. For example, where a writer uses the authorial or narrative *I*, we can safely infer the writer or the narrator is the person speaking. In such cases, the first instance of the first person pronoun has been marked as the node. No such assumption was made in the case of the ambiguous *we*.

It should be noted also that, in a sense, having to mark on a two-dimensional physical text forces a reader to search linearly for an actual, typographical node which surely does not match the actual processing by the mind in most cases. However, the end result (the found node) should be same.

When he was eleven years old, *1Abe-Lincolns* young body began to change. The juices and glands began to make a long, tall boy out of /1him/. As the months and years went by, /1he/ noticed /1his/ lean wrists getting longer, /1his/ legs, too, and /1he/ was now looking over the heads of other boys, *2men* said.

As /1he/ took on more length, /2they/ said /1he/ was shooting up into the air like green corn in the summer of a good corn-year. So /1he/ grew. When /1he/ reached seventeen years of age, and /0they/ measured /1him/, /1he was six feet, nearly four inches, high, from the bottom of /1his/ moccasins to the top of /1his/ skull.

Figure 3.1. Reader-marking of Text for Computer Input.

Essentially, the programs first define appropriate terms; then they identify each word of each text as a node, a cohesive element, or a "general word" and count the total number of words. After identification and counting of each node and cohesive element encountered sequentially, the computer assigns a word location number and places them in appropriate tables and arrays. Finally, the distance between each element and its node is calculated.

Summary statistics from the SNOBOL4 programs for each segment analyzed include:

- the total number of words
- the total number of nodes
- the total number of nodes as a percentage the total number of words
- the total number of occurrences of cohesive elements
- the total number of cohesive elements as a percentage of the total number of words
- the total number of occurrences of unfulfilled cohesive elements
- the total number of unfulfilled cohesive elements as a percentage of the total number of words

These statistics serve two functions. One, they allow us to look at the relative numbers of the phenomenon being studied to discern variation (or lack of it) in text-types; and two, they can be used as input for further processing.

The second or graphic part of the computer analysis has four functions. The first is to discern if the visual patterns formed by cohesive networks appear to verify the statistical results or to discern if variation in cohesion exists which the statistics do not show. The second is to show graphically the pattern in text often referred to in the literature (as suggested in Chapter 1.) At the same time it suggests graphically the complexities of the mind's processing of cohesion. The fourth function is to provide input to show the rudiments of texture in text.

These goals are accomplished through a FORTRAN/PL-1 plot program, into which location data from the SNOBOL4 program results are entered. Essentially, the plot program instructs the computer to draw a line between each cohesive element and its node (i.e., the cohesive ties). The configuration of the results, in general, is a set of networks, each formed by a node with lines radiating to the associated cohesive elements. The resulting 'maps' are a graphic representation of the cohesive networks in each text segment. (The numerical data are discussed in the next chapter, as are the maps.)

The plotting procedure requires abstracting the texts by adopting an arbitrary word length of six letters to the word and an arbitrary line length of twelve words (e.g., a text of 870 words would be 72 full lines and a part of a line). Thus, each map is laid out on a nonvisible grid with rows of twelve uniform horizontal cells and a column length which is a function of the total number of words in each text divided by twelve.[31]

For the pronouns and definite articles, the computer is instructed to draw a circle for the node from which a line is drawn to a small dot representing the element. For the agent displacements, the computer draws a circle for a present participle node with a star for its element and a square for a past participle node with a dot for its element. A single node may in a few cases serve more than one kind of verbal cohesive element and thus be marked with both a circle and a square. Cohesive elements having ambiguous or nonexplicit nodes appear as single black dot symbols.[32]

The relative locations of sentence endings, paragraph boundaries, and pagination might add graphic interest, but they are not shown because they may be confusing and they are not relevant to the problem at hand. The resulting maps are approximately 800–1400 words of running text. The map of the Sandburg text cited above is shown in Figure 3.2 below. Here the words (nodes and cohesive elements) are shown although they do not appear in the computer plots; also, nonrelevant words are represented by a dot though such dots do not appear on the maps because they could easily be confused with cohesive elements having no explicit node.

The set of three maps for each text constitutes a first visualization of the numerical data from the SNOBOL4 programs.[33]

A final step in the analysis developed for this research transfers the cohesive networks for the three types of cohesion in each text to three shades of gray. The "sum" of each set as overlays displays the unique texture for each text. Chapter 4 looks at the results of these analyses in the light of the initial hypotheses.

---

[31] Neither word length nor line length was deemed to be relevant to the problem at hand: therefore, the arbitrary lengths do not affect the results. It can, of course, be argued that abstracting the text in this way causes distortion in itself, but the skewing caused by presenting linear data on a two-dimensional map does not affect either the number of ties or the distances spanned and so is irrelevant to the findings. I should note also that while there may be some advantages to retaining the words of the text along with the constructed networks (rather than displaying empty cells), it would be disadvantageous if the map is to be easily read.

[32] For the set of maps for definite articles, it is the noun in the noun phrase rather than the definite article to which the line is drawn and it is the location of the noun which is determined,. This was done because it is the noun which is associated with the node and because the resulting data are more informative than having all cohesive elements listed as *the*.

[33] A decision was made in the mapping process to include only those pronouns having three or more cohesive elements (along with, of course, unfulfilled cohesive elements). This was done to reduce the complexity of maps such as Sandburg 1, Hemingway 1, Porter, White, and Clark 2 so that they would be reasonably readable. Had this same decision been applied to definite articles and agent displacements, these maps would have shown very little cohesion.

Analyzing Patterns of Cohesion 53

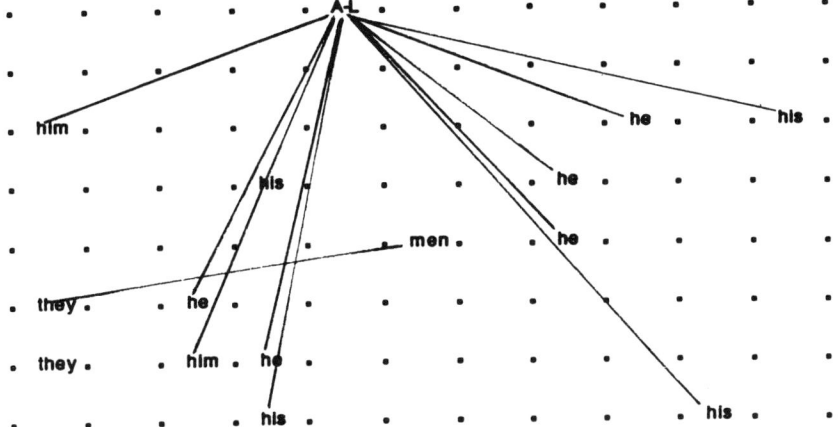

Figure 3.2. Map Spacing of Nodes and Cohesive Elements.

4
Cohesion as a Component of Texture

Previous systematic studies of the nature of texts have succeeded only in limited ways partly because of the complexity of the problem space, "text." Adequately accounting for this complexity will not be easy. If there is a "text" which is other than a physical text, there must be defining characteristics or commonalities that allow us to categorize its members in this way. These, in the aggregate, define the problem space "text." One of these characteristics of texts is "texture." Although others in the field have not defined "texture" as I have in Chapter 1,[1] is it not possible that this is what Halliday and Hasan (1976) sensed when they included a "direction-distance" factor in their encoding of the description of cohesion? Or what Grimes (1975) was working toward in developing his Thurman charts of discourse information? Or what Sedelow and Sedelow (1966, p. 2) mean when they say:

> Natural language invariably contains stylistic (structural) patterns. These patterns serve as clues to the methods used to encode and to transmit information; they may also be used to help detect information structured to elicit certain responses.

While the Sedelows' view here is limited to structural patterns, they do suggest that text patterns are something more than simply occurrences. They are related to synergism and hence affect communication.

Texture, by its very nature, is spatial. In the case of texts, the spatiality is initially provided by the physical text and is the result of potentially many text-forming patterns. Determining the spatial nature of those patterns will help us to understand certain characteristics they have in common and the ways they contribute to texture. The patterns formed by networks of cohesion provide a test case.

One way of discerning patterns, of course, is to rely on statistical evidence,

---

[1] I believe, for instance, that even typologies such as Christopherson's (1939), Hawkins' (1978), and Clark's (1975) are based on patterns of occurrences that these researchers perceived—perhaps without realizing the contribution of patterns to texture.

a tool often used by social scientists, including some linguists.[2] However, an overreliance on statistics alone is deceptive unless they are coupled with insights into writer and reader strategies, the latter being basic to the definition of text. It is particularly difficult to present and adequately discuss the results from this research on cohesion because of the sheer quantity of statistics generated and because the statistics raise questions which are presently unanswered.

In this first approach to the problem of texture, only one reader-subject participated. Nevertheless, for that reader's perceptions, the resulting data are promising in the light of Hypothesis I and Hypothesis II which look at the relative number of cohesive patterns and the relative cohesiveness perceived in texts. Furthermore, the numerical results are useful as map input data to visualize how a reader experiences texture, as suggested in Hypothesis III. The results of testing each hypothesis are discussed in some detail below.

THE INCIDENCE OF COHESION

Hypothesis I states that we would expect to find certain regularities in the occurrences of cohesive ties across all texts regardless of text-type. While the hypothesis might seem to be validated intuitively, there is much to be gained from looking at an actual reader's connections.

The computer data generated from reader-markings of individual texts are reported in Tables A-O in Appendix B. Each of these tables shows the initial numerical data for one of the three types of cohesion in one of the five categories of texts. (The column headings are explained on the page preceding Table A.) In general, this data includes the total number of words in each text, the number of nodes, the number of cohesive elements including both fulfilled and unfulfilled with the data subdivided for the two types of agent displacements. In addition, the tables show the percentages of (a) nodes to total words in each text (b) cohesive elements to number of words and (c) unfulfilled cohesive elements to the number of potential cohesive elements.

From these data, relevant summary statistics are shown in Tables 4.1, 4.2, and 4.3.[3] In general, these statistics compare occurrences of words, nodes, and cohesive elements (both fulfilled and unfulfilled) for all texts in each category of text. The occurrences shown in each summary table are discussed

---

[2] For example, the articles by Gibson (1970), Hayes (1970), Halliday (1970), and Milic (1970) employ statistical analyses.

[3] The order in which the text-types are listed is deliberate, based on my initial intuition about their relative cohesiveness. That is, I assumed that the texts would range from nonfiction as the least cohesive to short stories as the most cohesive. This intuition was based mainly on my experience of texts prior to the calculation of the statistical results.

below in greater detail. The medians given in Tables 4.1–4.3 are those for the percentages of each text-type as shown in Appendix B, Table A–O.[4]

Table 4.1: Number of nodes relative to length of text (in %). In Table 4.1, the first column shows the percentage of occurrences of definite article nodes for all texts in each genre compared to the total number of words (Def Nodes/Words), the second column the same statistic for pronoun nodes (Pro Nodes/Words), and the third for agent displacements (AgD Nodes/Words). These are perhaps the least interesting of the numerical data. In the first place, the percentage of nodes in all text-types is very small. In no genre does this figure exceed 4 percent of the total words (although in some individual texts it does). In fact, there is an amazing consistency in these data, yet a few divergences are apparent. For instance, the percentage of definite article nodes in nonfiction is twice that of nodes for short stories (the highest and lowest). The reverse is true of the pronoun nodes in nonfiction and short stories (the lowest and highest) although the percentage of short story nodes is not quite twice the percentage of nonfiction nodes.[5] This reversal is not at all unexpected in light of the fact that the subject matter of nonfiction often does not involve people.

It appears from these statistics that the number of cohesion nodes introduced for 20th-century American texts is relatively small and reasonably consistent across all text-types. Therefore, although Hypothesis I is tenta-

Table 4.1. Number of Nodes Relative to Length of Text (in %)

	Def Nodes/Words	Pro Nodes/Words	AgD Nodes/Words
Nonfiction	3.86	1.69	1.58
Median	3.93	1.60	1.62
Essay	3.17	1.79	1.57
Median	2.93	1.80	1.39
Biography	3.12	2.63	1.74
Median	2.82	2.39	1.78
Novel	2.29	2.47	1.23
Median	2.38	2.26	1.28
Short Story	1.91	3.03	1.48
Median	1.91	2.65	1.62

Source: By Author

---

[4] Because the aim of this study was to explore the problem of space, I dealt with descriptive statistics rather than trying to determine the significance of the differences.

[5] The SNOBOL4 computer program I wrote does not account for the fact that some nodes in some texts are repeated (reentry). Had it allowed for such, the picture here might be altered somewhat. See Chapter 2 for further discussion of reentry.

tively confirmed[6] as regards the occurrence of nodes in texts, we might look at some reasons why there are so few. There may be a "negative" syntactic explanation that the proportionately larger number of occurrences of all other categories of words may keep the percentage of nodes small. I think it more likely, however, that a pragmatic explanation better fits the case: the limitations of readers' minds. That is, a reader presumably processes every node and its various associated cohesive elements, and there may well be a physiological and psychological limit to the numbers which can be processed.[7] While this explanation is plausible, it cannot be accepted until further testing is done.

Table 4.2 Number of Cohesive Elements Relative to Length of Text (in %). For the percentages of occurrences of cohesive elements for all texts in each genre compared to the total number of words, the results reported in Table 4.2 exhibit somewhat more variation than those in Table 4.1. These data show two types of information: (a) the percentage for all texts in each text-type and (b) the median percentage for each text-type. The first, third, and fifth columns show all cohesive elements of each type as a percentage of the total number of words. The second, fourth, and sixth columns give the percentages for only the fulfilled cohesive elements.

Table 4.2. Number of Cohesive Elements Relative to Length of Text (in %)

	Def CE/ Words	Def FCE/ Words	Pro CE/ Words	Pro FCE/ Words	AgD CE/ Words	AgD FCE/ Words
Nonfiction	14.40	11.84	4.11	2.97	4.00	2.21
Median	15.00		3.38		3.90	
Essay	14.84	12.56	6.50	5.84	3.32	1.99
Median	14.78		6.59		3.18	
Biography	13.10	9.74	7.89	7.59	3.40	2.51
Median	12.04		7.45		3.12	
Novel	12.68	8.74	10.48	9.60	2.73	1.83
Median	12.84		9.80		2.68	
Short Story	11.22	8.54	10.95	10.05	2.63	2.08
Median	11.64		11.02		2.72	

Source: By Author

---

[6] The generality of validation must remain tentative at this juncture until the results of a wider test sample confirm or disconfirm them.

[7] Indeed, this may be why some readers have difficulty with certain books by Russian authors which introduce innumerable characters, each of which is a potential cohesive node.

In every category, there is a difference between all cohesive elements and those that are fulfilled. This means that, generally speaking, all text-types have some cohesion-nodes that are not explicit (though Table-O, Appendix B, show some individual passages to be exceptions). Furthermore, since the percentage of each text devoted to network-forming elements is necessarily equal to or greater than the number of nodes, we would expect the figures in Table 4.2 to be larger than those in Table 4.1 in every category, as in fact they are.

Of the three types of cohesion, the agent displacement category shows the lowest percentages of occurrence in all text-types, with none as high as either of the other categories of cohesion (i.e., comparing fulfilled only or comparing total only) within a text-type. Furthermore, there is very little variation in the percentage of occurrence of agent displacement in the five types. This means that, while all of the text-types do employ agent displacement, it does not appear to be very useful as a cohesive device in any of them. Striving for variation in syntactic structure in sentences may limit its occurrence, but the lower percentage may also be due to readers having more difficulty in processing agent displacements.

On the other hand, for pronoun cohesion, it is not surprising that short stories and novels show percentages more than twice those of nonfiction, given the fact that virtually all personal pronouns are edited out of most nonfiction work.[8] This fact suggests the greater dependence on pronouns in novels and short stories. In both cases, the overall percentage is more than twice that of nonfiction. While the essay category appears to support my placement of it as being most like nonfiction and biography, this statistic may be deceptive. If the essay category is divided into personal essays and expository essays,[9] the percentage of pronouns for the four personal essays increases from 6.50 percent to 8.53 percent thus becoming greater than that for biographies and more like that for novels. The percentage for the remaining essays decreases from 6.50 percent to 3.32 percent to be more like other types of nonfiction.

The definite articles present a methodological problem which does not affect the other types of cohesion. That is, the marking system by which the computer identified the cohesive elements included only one word of the definite noun phrase (i.e., the noun and not the definite article itself). Hence, the original data (shown in Tables A-E, Appendix B) reflects only half the number of words really involved in definite article cohesion. In order to compensate for this, I corrected for this by doubling the percentage for definite noun phrases in Table 4.2 to show the *actual* number of words

---

[8] The text by Matthiessen is a notable exception to this "rule" in the nonfiction books analyzed here.

[9] The essays by Didion, Eiseley, Thurber, and White are classed as personal; those by Friedman, Talese, and Thomsen are classed as expository.

directly involved as cohesive elements. This adjustment significantly increases the percentage of words for the definite article category. Thus, the definite articles and their associated nouns in every category of text account for a greater percentage of the total words than do the others.[10] (An alternate choice would have been to consider the definite article and its noun as one word which would then distort the total number of words.)

The range of frequency of occurrence of definite articles and agent displacements across text-types is much narrower than the range for pronouns. Furthermore, the percentages of definite articles and agent displacements between text-types gradually decrease in the order given, from nonfiction to short story; at the same time, the percentages for pronouns increase from nonfiction to short story. Comparing percentages of pronouns and definite noun phrases in the same type shows that in short stories the figures are similar, but the percentage of definites in essay texts is over twice that of pronouns, and for nonfiction texts, it is two-and-a-half times the percentage of pronouns in the same type. This suggests that short stories rely about equally on pronouns and definites, but essays and nonfiction make much greater use of definite articles than pronouns. This is not perhaps unexpected, given the diminished emphasis on people in most nonfiction texts and essays.

Obviously, the statistics reported in Table 4.2 are neither startling nor totally uninteresting. Their importance here is that they further confirm Hypothesis 1 by showing that cohesive elements exist in all five types of texts, but their range of occurrence within and between text-types is greater than that for the nodes.

Table 4.3: Number of unfulfilled cohesive elements relative to all cohesive elements (in %). The last table of summary statistics shows the comparison of unfulfilled cohesive elements with all cohesive elements in each genre. The first column gives the percentages for the definite articles (Def UCE/CE), the second for the pronouns (Pro UCE/CE), the third for passive agent displacements (AgD UCEP/CE) and the fourth for *-ing* agent displacements (AgD UCEI/CE). These figures do not account for the fact that there may have been logically inferrable agent-nodes which the reader did not find explicit in the written text. In some future testing of readers, it would be useful and perhaps revealing to find a method to account for such.

The results, in contrast to those in Table 4.1 and 4.2, are quite striking for their seeming idiosyncrasies. Why, for instance, is there so much variation within columns and within rows, and why don't the high and low percentages in each column follow the patterns seen in Table 4.2? Clearly, agent displacements are less like the other two cohesion categories. Still, some generalizations can be made.

A first generalization is that, by dividing the agent displacements into

---

[10] Does this mean, then that this type of cohesion has a greater effect on the readers' perceptions of cohesiveness?

Table 4.3. Number of Unfulfilled Cohesive Elements Relative to All Cohesive Elements (in %)

		Def UCE/CE	Pro UCE/CE	AgD UCEP/CE	AgD UCEI/CE
Nonfiction		17.74	27.66	72.33	19.05
	Median	13.89	26.42	67.65	16.22
Essay		15.43	10.13	75.56	13.33
	Median	16.28	9.47	75.00	10.34
Biography		25.63	3.80	66.00	6.01
	Median	27.43	3.21	65.79	6.25
Novel		31.14	8.81	66.24	10.78
	Median	29.47	10.12	69.23	9.09
Short Story		23.94	8.21	53.76	2.89
	Median	22.22	7.02	50.00	4.55

Source: By Author

passives and *-ings*, we can see that the percentage of unfulfilled passives in every text-type is at least 50 percent and for both nonfiction and essays it is over 70 percent. (For some individual texts, the percentages reach 100%, according to Table K-O, Appendix B.) Obviously, it is quite common to have a passive verb or verbal without an explicit node, but at the same time it must be noted that the percentage of total occurrences of agent displacements cohesive ties is relatively low.[11]

Like the passives, the percentage of total occurrences of *-ing* verbals is relatively low, but here again, both nonfiction and essays seem more likely to have unfulfilled cohesive elements than the other text-types. In fact, the percentage for nonfiction is more than six times that for short stories and the percentage for essays is more than four times that for short stories.

A second kind of generalization about unfulfilled cohesive elements can be made from the fact that the percentage of unfulfilled pronouns is very high for nonfiction, being over seven times that for biography, three times that for short stories, and over twice as large as for essays (the second largest percentage in this column). The percentage of unfulfilled agent displacements and pronouns for nonfiction and essays shows them to be appreciably higher than for the other categories of texts. The editorial *we* which is the most common "permissible" pronoun in many types of nonfiction may account for a good share of these because its node is often ambiguous or extratextual.

---

[11] The data here provide ample validation for the arguments of Stanley (Penelope) and Wolfe (Robbins) (1977) in their discussion and refutation of Chomsky's recoverability condition (1964, p. 71).

In contrast to this observation, a third generalization is evident, namely, that a comparison of numerical data for the unfulfilled definite articles in nonfiction and essays shows them to be appreciably fewer than the other types of cohesion. Perhaps this can be explained by a greater need to be explicit in writing about more abstract subjects. If this is the case, apparently this same need for explicitness does not hold for pronoun and agent recovery in nonfiction and essays as cited above. Almost the reverse is true for biography where the pronouns are almost always retrievable, but the percentage of unfulfilled definite articles is relatively high. These apparent differences in usage of unfulfilled cohesion provide important information about differences among text-types. These differences apparently hinge on the assumptions writers make about their readers' knowledge or on the relative importance writers attach to the need for precision in interpretation.

Thus, the statistics reported in Table 4.3, while seemingly idiosyncratic, do show that there is differentiation among the five text-types as regards the usage of unfulfilled cohesion. Nevertheless, all types employ all types of unfulfilled cohesion and do so with some degree of consistency, further confirming Hypothesis I.

In summary, the numerical patterns of occurrences of nodes and cohesive elements show that the potential for cohesion is a characteristic of all written texts analyzed here. While regularities are evident, the greatest variation is exhibited in the comparison of unfulfilled cohesive elements to all cohesive elements. By revealing cohesion data in actual, as opposed to contrived, texts, these statistical results add to our tentative knowledge of the problem space "text."

THE RELATIVENESS OF COHESION

We might predict that reading can be accomplished more efficiently if all parts of a written text are sufficiently related to all other parts (a quantity yet to be determined); one way of looking at some of the relationships that hold is to examine the way cohesive ties operate to aid a person's reading. Specifically, if a reader's mind is required by a cohesive element to retrieve a node that appears, say, eight paragraphs previously, the reader is more likely to find a relationship between the two sections of the written text than if no such tie-potential existed. We might also expect published writers to understand this need. However, merely determining the relative number of occurrences of perceived cohesive ties is not enough to help us understand how cohesion operates to unify a text (even if the data for all 56 passages included in this study were tested by multiple subjects and probability statistics tabulated from the results). Occurrence data are important, but the unity of a text of more than a few sentences also depends on ties which span chunks of texts larger than mere paragraphs. These global relationships add to the synergism of a text.

Hypothesis II says that the relative cohesiveness of a text is a function of the number of cohesive ties and the distances between the ends of cohesive ties. By calculating the average distance spanned by the several cohesion networks in each text, we can sense a writer's overall utilization of distance to build relationships; likewise, by calculating the average number of cohesive elements per node, we can sense how tightly focused each text is.[12] An index of cohesion can be formulated by multiplying the average distance by the average number of occurrences for each segment of each text. A more complex index which might be devised to account for intersection and reentry as well as frequency of occurrence and distance would probably be even more revealing of reader processing. Nevertheless, this initial exploratory index is promising.

A simple and convenient way of expressing distance is by noting the locations of tie-terminals and counting the number of words intervening between them (i.e., between each element and its node). It should be noted, however, that it is not the location of a cohesive element per se that is important in giving us a sense of a text being unitary; rather, it is the cumulative effect of many tie-lengths spanning a written passage.

A comparison of Tables P–T (Appendix B with column headings explained on the page preceding Table A) shows considerable variation in the average distances across all texts and text-types, with the agent displacements generally covering shorter distances than pronouns and definite articles. At the same time, there is apparently less variation in the average number of cohesive elements per node although the pronoun averages are generally larger than those of the other two types of cohesion and very few individual averages exceed five per node.

From these data, cohesion indexes are calculated by multiplying the average number of ties by the average distance (i.e., the data given in Tables P–T). Tables 4.4 through 4.8 present the cohesion index for all three types of cohesion for all texts. The first column displays the calculated cohesion index for definite articles (Def CI) in each text of each type, the second that for pronouns (Pro CI), and the third for agent displacements (AgD CI). These cohesion indexes show variation because a variation in the average number of ties and/or the average distance will cause a corresponding variation in the index of cohesion.

These results reflect the reading of one subject; theoretically, an index of cohesion can be calculated for each reader. If the text-type classification used here is valid, there should be a reasonable consistency in these individual

---

[12] For the 13 maps shown in Figures 4.5–4.17 statistical results of these averages are reported in Tables P–T in Appendix B.

Table 4.4. Cohesion Index-Nonfiction

	Def CI	Pro CI	AgD CI
Baker/Allen 1	72.09	12.33	41.97
Baker/Allen 2	28.76	12.38	19.21
Lakoff 1	33.78	120.52	18.63
Lakoff 2	49.10	5.95	15.76
Matthiessen 1	84.84	361.67	10.75
Matthiessen 2	35.43	892.78	18.35
Sagan 1	131.08	64.68	46.09
Sagan 2	82.02	11.61	23.00
Silverberg 1	59.08	25.80	15.60
Silverberg 2	35.23	11.97	33.30
Skinner 1	34.00	14.07	20.63
Skinner 2	23.35	37.98	4.67
Stoddard 1	73.02	11.23	4.80
Stoddard 2	137.06	60.30	212.04
All Texts	64.09	133.97	35.12

Source: By Author

cohesion indexes for all readers. If we find in future testing that this is not the case, we will have to determine if the measure is faulty or if the type-classifications (when evaluated by the measure of cohesion, at least) need revision.

While it is not possible to do an exhaustive analysis of the resulting data, I will consider three levels of interpretation. The first level looks at within-text-type differences; the second considers between-text-type differences; and the third examines cohesion category differences.

Table 4.5. Cohesion Index-Essay

	Def CI	Pro CI	AgD CI
Didion	32.05	2559.23	77.59
Eiseley	257.28	1860.15	9.96
Friedman	263.78	222.24	24.92
Talese	45.81	50.31	6.69
Thomsen	168.53	18.50	14.85
Thurber	154.92	1536.86	26.26
White	273.17	1146.65	9.92
All Texts	186.46	1076.19	23.30

Source: By Author

Table 4.6. Cohesion Index-Biography

	Def CI	Pro CI	AgD CI
Angelou 1	123.05	342.86	32.87
Angelou 2	30.50	484.60	14.07
Gray 1	24.89	599.15	371.52
Gray 2	57.61	25.71	18.92
Haley 1	42.31	1447.65	16.91
Haley 2	19.90	1043.36	17.83
Hodge 1	37.66	46.85	15.10
Hodge 2	46.18	41.94	13.51
Milford 1	173.35	42.17	5.17
Milford 2	205.23	44.09	41.18
Sandburg 1	35.89	583.29	157.03
Sandburg 2	15.73	92.39	45.61
Sandoz 1	45.49	62.09	11.09
Sandoz 2	97.97	85.23	16.19
All Texts	70.98	358.16	50.37

Source: By Author

Within-text-type differences. If, for example, the average number of definite articles per node and the average distance for definite articles are approximately the same, as they are in Lakoff 1 (1.27 and 26.60 respectively, in Table P) and Skinner 1 (1.28 and 26.56 respectively, Table P), the cohesion indexes for these two segments will be very similar, as in fact they are (33.78 and 34.00 respectively, Table 4.4). This says that, based on these segments alone, we might predict that these two nonfiction texts are very similar in their potential for definite article cohesion.

On the other hand, if the average number of pronouns per node is about the same, as in London 1 and Lee 2 (3.55 and 3.57 respectively, Table S), but the average pronoun distances contrast greatly, as happens in this case where London's is almost twice that of Lee's (149.05 and 78.00 respectively, Table S), the cohesion indexes for these segments will also contrast as indeed they do, with an index of 529.13 for London and an index of 278.46 for Lee (Table 4.7). It appears that in these novels London makes more use of distance to unify his text while using about the same number of pronouns. Thus for pronouns in these segments at least, London 1 appears to be more cohesive than Lee 2.

Still another possible combination of variability occurs where the average distances are relatively the same but the average number of cohesive elements varies, in which case the cohesion indexes will also be different. The definite

Table 4.7. Cohesion Index-Novel

	Def CI	Pro CI	AgD CI
Clark 1	103.54	358.86	109.96
Clark 2	18.00	1764.24	879.66
Fitzgerald 1	27.04	1566.96	5.39
Fitzgerald 2	75.32	767.07	13.82
Hemingway 1	365.37	327.89	44.56
Hemingway 2	63.84	1098.39	8.60
Kesey 1	104.66	686.81	117.82
Kesey 2	376.53	142.14	153.62
Lee 1	95.26	307.09	5.49
Lee 2	21.68	278.46	218.54
London 1	278.30	529.13	14.31
London 2	292.38	300.45	33.45
Safire 1	503.76	161.14	37.25
Safire 2	53.07	54.70	17.37
All Text	184.34	556.86	101.81

Source: By Author

Table 4.8. Cohesion Index-Short Story

	Def CI	Pro CI	AgD CI
Bradbury	270.10	149.87	30.28
Faulkner	783.93	434.34	11.38
Hammett	283.72	79.13	14.74
O'Connor	146.36	114.71	9.07
Porter	52.82	429.71	249.61
Rivers	441.46	1873.02	63.64
Steinbeck	333.87	185.32	47.78
All Texts	347.92	432.03	54.43

Source: By Author

articles in Angelou 2 and Sandoz 1 are a case in point where the average distance for Angelou is 22.10 words and the average number of cohesive elements is 1.38 per node (Table R) and Sandoz has an average distance of 22.40 words and an average of 2.03 cohesive elements per node (Table R). This means that the cohesion index for Sandoz's definite articles is half again as much as Angelou's (45.49 compared to 30.50 respectively, Table 4.6). It is clear that Sandoz uses definite articles as cohesive devices (in this work, at least) more often than Angelou. This raises several issues. For one thing, we might conjecture that because of this Sandoz's segment can be read more efficiently than Angelou's, but too many factors are yet to be determined, such as consistency.

The question of a writer's consistency in using a particular type of cohesion is exemplified in Table 4.6 which shows that the definite article cohesion index for the second segment of Sandoz's work is more than twice that of the first while the same index in Angelou's work is four times as large in the first segment as in the second. Obviously, definite article use must be related to subject matter. Is the subject matter in the two segments of each writer's work really so different? Or, is the treatment of it so inconsistent? In looking at these writers' other works, would we find them as seemingly inconsistent? How do these differences affect the overall texture of these passages? These are unanswered (and perhaps unanswerable) questions at this time.

If a particular text appears to be much more cohesive than another text when compared according to cohesion type, it does not necessarily mean that that text will be more cohesive overall. In the case of Sandoz 1 and Angelou 2, for instance, when the pronoun and agent displacement indexes are added to the definite article index, the total for Angelou's text is over four times as large as Sandoz's (529.17 compared to 118.67 as calculated from Table 4.6). Factoring in all types of cohesion might produce greater or lesser differences (although the three types considered here probably have the greatest potential for distance and in the case of the pronouns and definite articles, the greatest potential for occurrence). Many comparisons could be made for other segments as well, but looking at the several text-types holistically will be useful at this point.

The variations within a text-type raise interesting questions. For instance, Matthiessen's book (Table 4.4) shows unusually high indexes for pronouns compared to the other nonfiction texts. The total indexes for both segments of Matthiessen (457.26 and 946.56) greatly exceed the cohesion index for all nonfiction texts (233.18 in Table 4.9). This may be explained by the fact that *The Snow Leopard* is journal-like and, hence, more autobiographical in nature than the other books analyzed in the nonfiction category. Was it, then, miscategorized as to text-type, or is the category, as presently constituted, simply too broad?

Another example of within-type differences is shown in Table 4.6 where we can see that Haley's use of pronouns far exceeds that of any other texts (an index of over 1000.00 in both segments). If *The Autobiography of Malcolm X* can be categorized as autobiography (even though Haley edited it), the question is raised whether a difference between biography and autobiography might explain the disparity. However, the only other autobiography in the set, Angelou's *I Know Why a Caged Bird Sings*, does not have comparable indexes (342.86 and 484.6). They are, in fact, lower than those for two biographies, Gray 1 (599.15) and Sandburg 1 (583.29). Do these results mean that Angelou's book is more like biography, or that Haley's book is an aberration? Or, is the difference due to Malcolm X's relating his life orally to Haley—a difference between pronoun usage in speech as opposed to writing (assuming Haley did little editing of Malcolm X's revelations)?

Between-text-type difference. The summary cohesion index calculated by multiplying the average distances for all texts in a genre by the average number of cohesive elements in the same texts and shown in Table 4.9 compares the data across text-types. The first column lists the summary cohesion index for definite article (Def SCI) in each type, the second for pronouns (Pro SCI), and the third for agent displacements (AgD SCI). The fourth column is the sum of three indexes for each text-type (ALL SCI). From these figures, we might speculate that comparative cohesion may be one criterion for defining text-types, or genres.

The data here are not unpredictable, based on the occurrence data and cohesion indexes for individual texts. By combining the cohesion indexes for each type, we can see that, as the numerical data predict, the nonfiction texts are the least cohesive (with an index of 233.18). Biographies are next (with an index of 479.51). As we might expect, the novels and short stories are very similar (with indexes of 843.01 and 834.38 respectively) and much more cohesive than nonfiction and biographies. Because the cohesion indexes for novels and short stories is so similar, these indexes do not differentiate between the types. If they are discrete text-types, the distinction must be based on other criteria.

We might have predicted that the reader would find the novels and short stories to be very cohesive, but to discover that they are not the most cohesive is quite surprising. What is even more surprising is the fact that the essay category (with an index of 1284.00) is the most cohesive, having an index half again greater than short stories and novels. On closer scrutiny, it is clear that the figure for the pronoun category is definitely skewed by the personal essays. By separating the essays into two categories—personal and exposi-

Table 4.9. Summary Cohesion Index

	Def SCI	Pro SCI	AgD SCI	All SCI
Nonfiction	64.09	133.97	35.12	233.18
Essay	186.46	1076.19	23.30	1284.00
Personal		1702.47		
Expository		80.94		
Biography	70.98	358.16	50.37	479.51
Novel	184.34	556.86	101.81	843.01
Short Story	347.92	432.03	54.43	834.38

Source: By Author

tory—and refiguring the pronoun index, the extent of this skewing is more obvious. For the expository essays, the cohesion index is 80.94 which is more like that of nonfiction texts; for personal essays the cohesion index is 1702.47 which is double that of novels and short stories. This may explained by the consistent use of the first person pronoun throughout the personal essays which perhaps, even though they are technically "non-fiction," makes them more like fiction than nonfiction. As the results here and on page 58 suggest, for this cohesion data at least, the text-type "essay" needs revision.

Cohesion categories. A third mode for interpreting results looks at cohesion categories. In Table 4.9, we can see that the agent displacement category is apparently the least effectively used and thus is the least powerful cohesive device. In contrast, the pronouns are clearly the most effectively used and the most useful for certain rhetorical reasons which were suggested earlier.

To summarize, the data discussed here tentatively confirm[13] the second hypothesis proposed in Chapter 1, namely, that the relative cohesiveness of a text is a function of the number of cohesive ties and the distance between the various nodes and their attendant cohesive elements. It is obvious that the preliminary occurrence statistics are of value not only for the information they convey but also as a basis for calculating the number of ties, the distances, and finally the cohesion indexes. While the numerical data provide us with an abundance of relevant information, there is still more to be learned from this examination of cohesion in texts.

THE VISUAL PATTERNING OF COHESION

This chapter began with speculation about the nature of patterns in texts and, more specifically, patterns of cohesion in texts. The text data analyzed here show that cohesion does create pattern, and they suggest that cohesion unifies a text by means of cohesive network patterns that span varying lengths of text passages. However, the results thus far reported do not fully determine the nature of cohesive patterns. The importance of the results lies in the fact that typologies and counting, when supplemented with other kinds of analyses, give us a better understanding of cohesion as it contributes to the texture of a text.

The fact that cohesive patterns are found in all texts and the fact that cohesiveness is relative in texts provide useful validations of our intuitions, but there is yet another way of verifying them. By translating some of the statistical information (i.e., location data) into mapping points, graphic depictions of cohesion patterns can be drawn. From these we can readily see how patterns of various texts resemble or differ from each other.

The computer can be programmed to represent cohesion networks graphically. In essence, these depictions represent the connections which the mind

---

[13] See Note 6 above.

Cohesion as a Component of Texture 69

makes between cohesive elements and their nodes. However, because we do not know exactly how the mind processes cohesive ties, graphic depictions at this stage must rely on logical assumptions. If the mind retrieves a node by testing each potential node in a linear manner as one might finger beads on a rosary, one after the other until an appropriate node is reached, the configuration of the pattern might be like that in Figure 4.3. On the other hand, if the mind makes some kind of direct association between each cohesive element and its node, the resulting pattern might resemble the network in Figure 4.4. In both figures, the circle represents the node word and each dot represents a cohesive element such as, say, a pronoun which may appear cataphorically or anaphorically in relation to its node.

Since we know that our eyes perceive words on the pages of a physical text one after another, the bead-string analogy is appealing. It is, after all, the way computer memories operate. Nevertheless, there are problems with this model. First, it would mean that the mind must "test" every word until an appropriate node is found. This kind of processing is very inefficient because the text would necessarily be scanned word by word multiple times. The opposite of this linear search would be to carry all words in short term memory until such time as they are needed. That is, having encountered a potential node once (in anaphoric cohesion), the mind might "carry it along" so that it would be present simultaneously when a cohesive element is subsequently encountered. If this were the case, however, all of the encountered words of a text would be at the "forefront" of the mind all the time ready for use at any time. The model envisioned in this case is simply too chaotic to imagine.

Second, in the Figure 4.3 model, if the mind were to encounter a cohesive element of the same type, previously identified (such as another pronoun with the same node), would the preceding one be the node of the following pronoun? Lakoff (1976, pp. 294-9) does not believe so. As he points out in the hierarchy of anaphora, an NP can't be the antecedent of another NP on the same level of definiteness; but, if the previous pronoun is already specified by a node, is it still on the same level of definiteness? If not, then the preceding pronoun can be an antecedent which seems illogical.

A third question regarding the efficacy of the bead-string model focuses

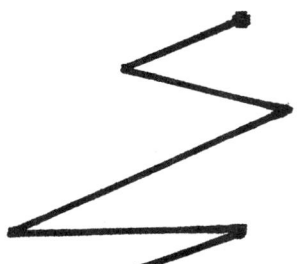 

Figure 4.3. Bead-string Model   **Figure 4.4. Network Model.**

on the problem of representing agent displacements. For instance, to process anaphoric cohesive elements, such as *cutting, burning, and piling* (Sandburg 1), in that order, a reader's mind, according to the bead-string analogy will first search linearly for and establish the agent of *cutting*, say, *Lincoln*. When it subsequently finds *burning*, it will follow the same path, reencountering *cutting* for which the node *Lincoln* will have already been established. Does the mind assume that both verbals have the same agent, or must it continue testing until all possible agents have been met and eliminated? In the case of all verbals in a series having the same node, the problem might be resolved without too much trouble, but not all verbals in a series will have the same agent necessitating extensive searching. (For instance, in the contrived sentence "Susan, *pleased* and *glowing*, exuded confidence," the agents of the verbals differ.) The inefficiency of such processing makes the bead-string analogy unattractive.

Although the computer-memory search model is still used as a model of human memory processing—largely because it is convenient—it is extremely doubtful that the mind follows such an inefficient path to create cohesiveness. Alternatively, Minsky's frame analysis and Gentner's Connectivity Hypothesis allow the possibility that we retrieve by "locating" semantically associated frames rather than by linear search. If this is true, then texts and texture can be looked at as multidimensional. Another kind of evidence for this is the fact that the mind can process several concepts at a time. For instance, the intersection of cohesion networks may require the mind to be searching for two or more nodes at the same time. The map of definite articles in Hemingway 1 (Figure 4.14) is a case in point. In a strictly linear search, this would be impossible.

For these reasons, I adopted the model in Figure 4.4, but even the model in Figure 4.4 is only a crude approximation of the real complexity of the mind's processing. Such a simplistic, two-dimensional diagram hardly qualifies as a wholly adequate representation of that process. Indeed, only when we begin to comprehend the mechanics of our mind's processing as we create texts will we be able to depict texts with some confidence.

One major problem not addressed by either Figure 4.3 or Figure 4.4 is that of the unfulfilled cohesive elements. If readers search futilely for an intratextual node, there is no way the models can account for a node inferred or created by a reader. The computer program used here simply counts these cohesive elements as unfulfilled. This only tells us, at a minimum, that a syntactically marked cohesive element exists and that a particular reader has not found an intratextual node; it does not reveal whether the reader has inferred or can infer an appropriate extratextual node or not. (Nor do we know whether all readers would make the same inference.) Furthermore, cohesive elements marked as unfulfilled do not indicate when a reader simply misses reading a node clearly available intratextually. Being able to differentiate between these possibilities would tell us even more about how readers process cohesion.

The diagrams or maps which I conceived based on the model in Figure 4.4 function in four principal ways:

1. To confirm or disconfirm the numerical data derived in the first phase of the computer analysis.
2. To reveal aspects of cohesion which the numerical data cannot.
3. To suggest the complexity of the mind's processing of cohesion.
4. To show the rudiments of texture created by the composite patterning of three types of cohesion.

One might argue that the computer mapping program (as described in Chapter 3) distorts the results and thus cannot function in these ways. While it is true that the program abstracts the physical text by systematizing the locations of the cohesive elements and nodes, it is also true that every physical text is in itself distorted because it is constrained to a limited line length and a limited number of lines per page which follow consecutively from left to right and top to bottom. Working with ink-formed words set down sequentially on a series of sheets of paper to represent the mind's processing has the same kinds of pitfalls that working with ink-formed musical notes on a score has in representing the tone of the human voice.

At some future time when we understand more about the multidimensionality of the mind's processing of texts, we may be able to represent cohesion and the texture of a text while circumventing these constraints, but in the meantime, we will have to live with what we can do. This does not mean that the maps have less value at this juncture; it simply means we can learn from them in spite of these shortcomings.[14] In any case, if we can trust our eyes to judge such functions, the maps clearly operate to provide information about texts that numerical data alone cannot. A case in point is the notion of intersection which was referred to in Chapter 2. The maps show very clearly the overlapping of cohesion networks, a fact we are hardly aware of as we read.

Because maps were generated for all 35 texts in the study including both segments of the longer texts, examining three different maps for each of the 56 segments would involve a rather complex analysis. Therefore, for presentation, I selected the computer maps for two texts in each genre, including both segments of one of the texts in each of the book-length text-types.[15] These maps are shown in Figures 4.5 through 4.17. The numerical data for

---

[14] It may be argued that to *abstract* these cohesion patterns from the physical text (i.e., to show them as straight lines while leaving out the printed words) overemphasizes the factor of location. It is the patterns themselves that are important as they contribute to the texture of a text.

[15] The maps presented here, while limited to 10 texts, are judged to be reasonably representative for purposes of explanation. The tables include the statistical information for all segments of all 35 texts.

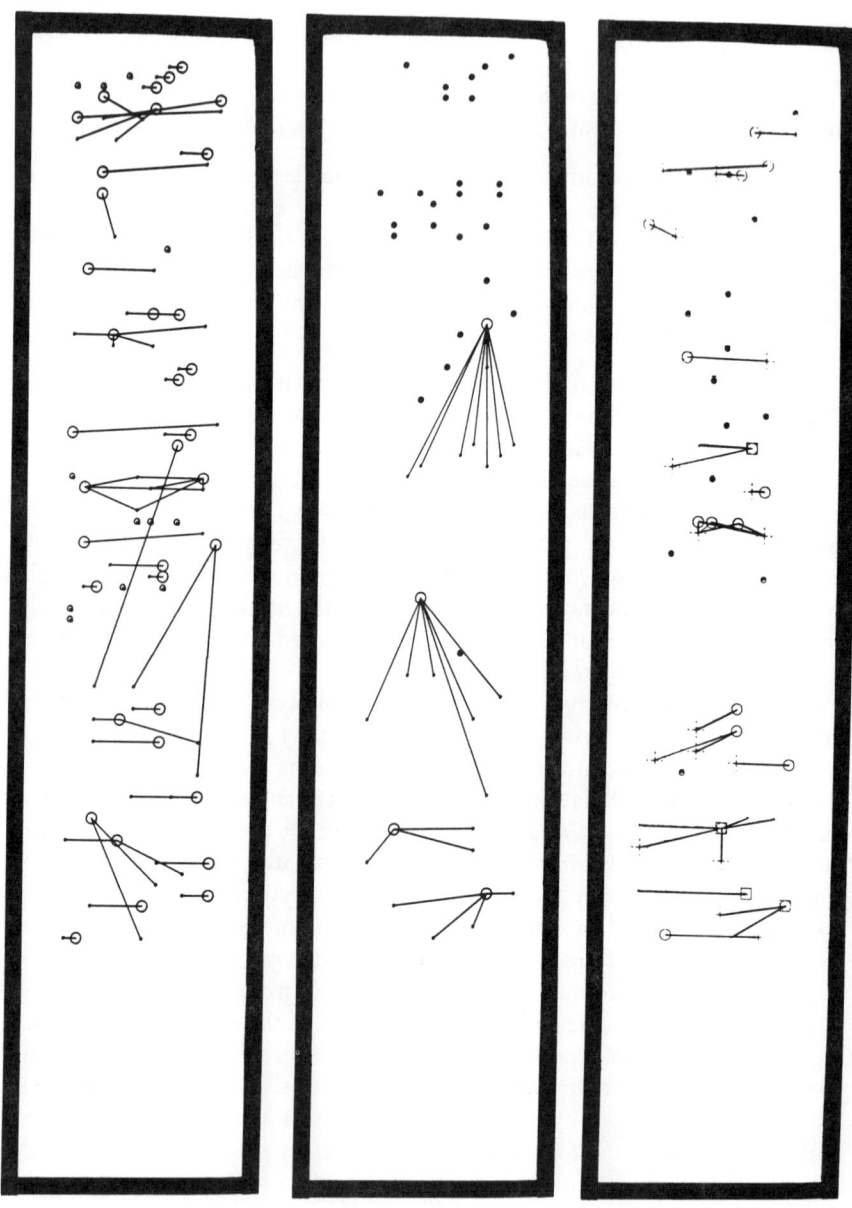

Figure 4.5. Lakoff 1, *Language and Woman's Place.*

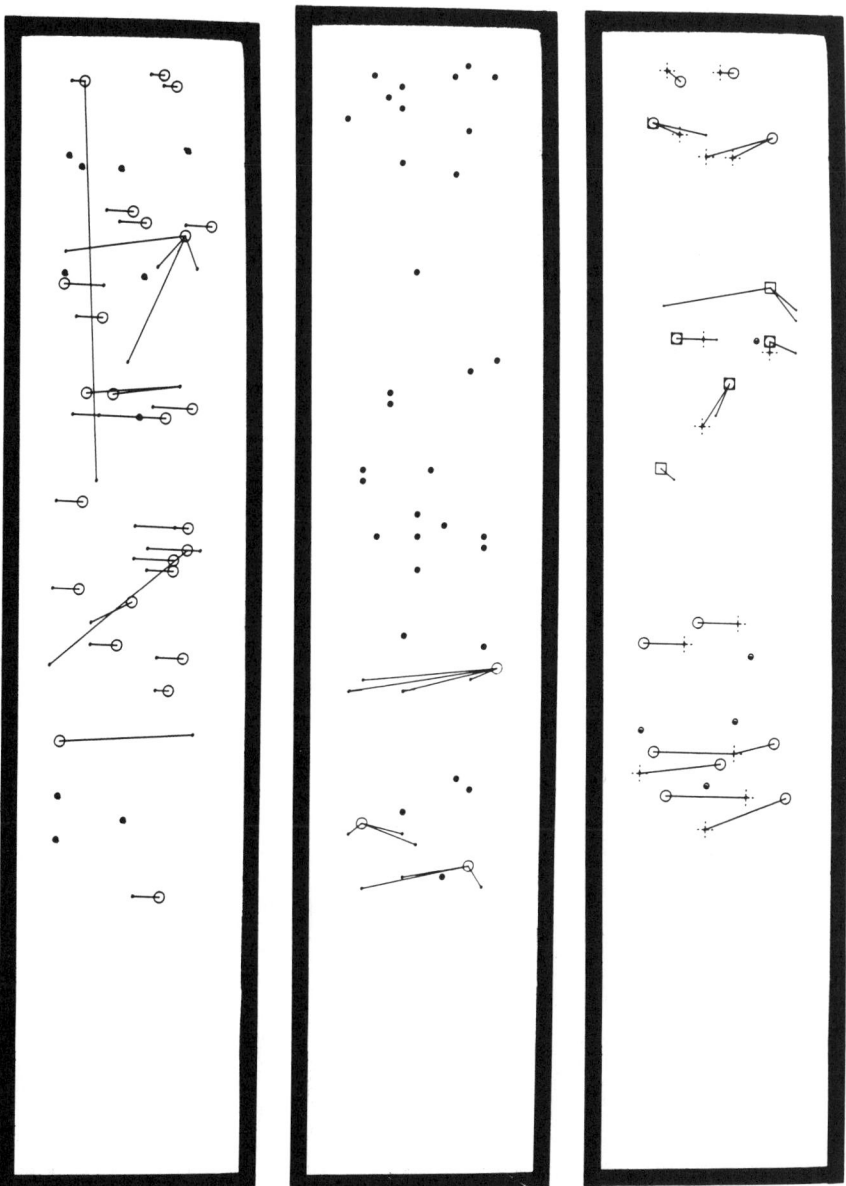

Figure 4.6. Skinner 1, *Beyond Freedom and Dignity.*

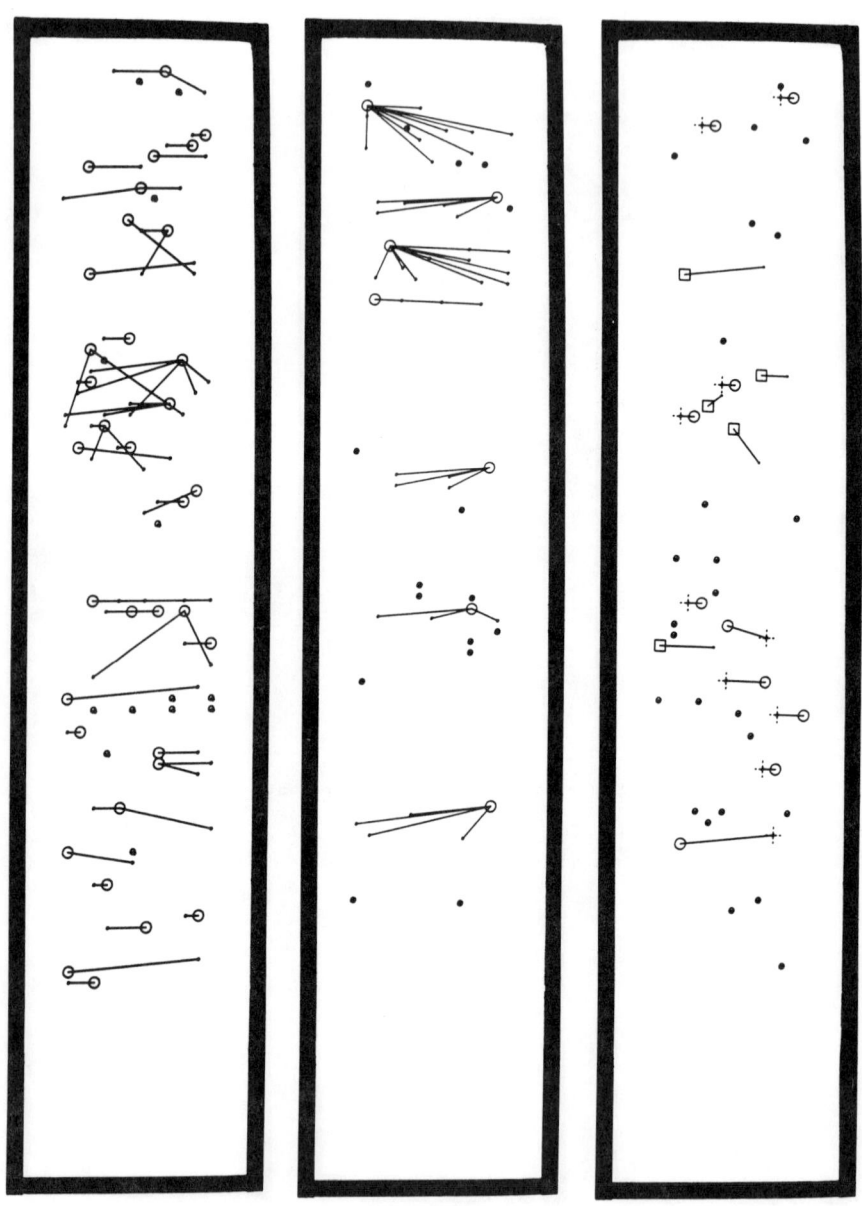

Figure 4.7. Skinner 2, *Beyond Freedom and Dignity*.

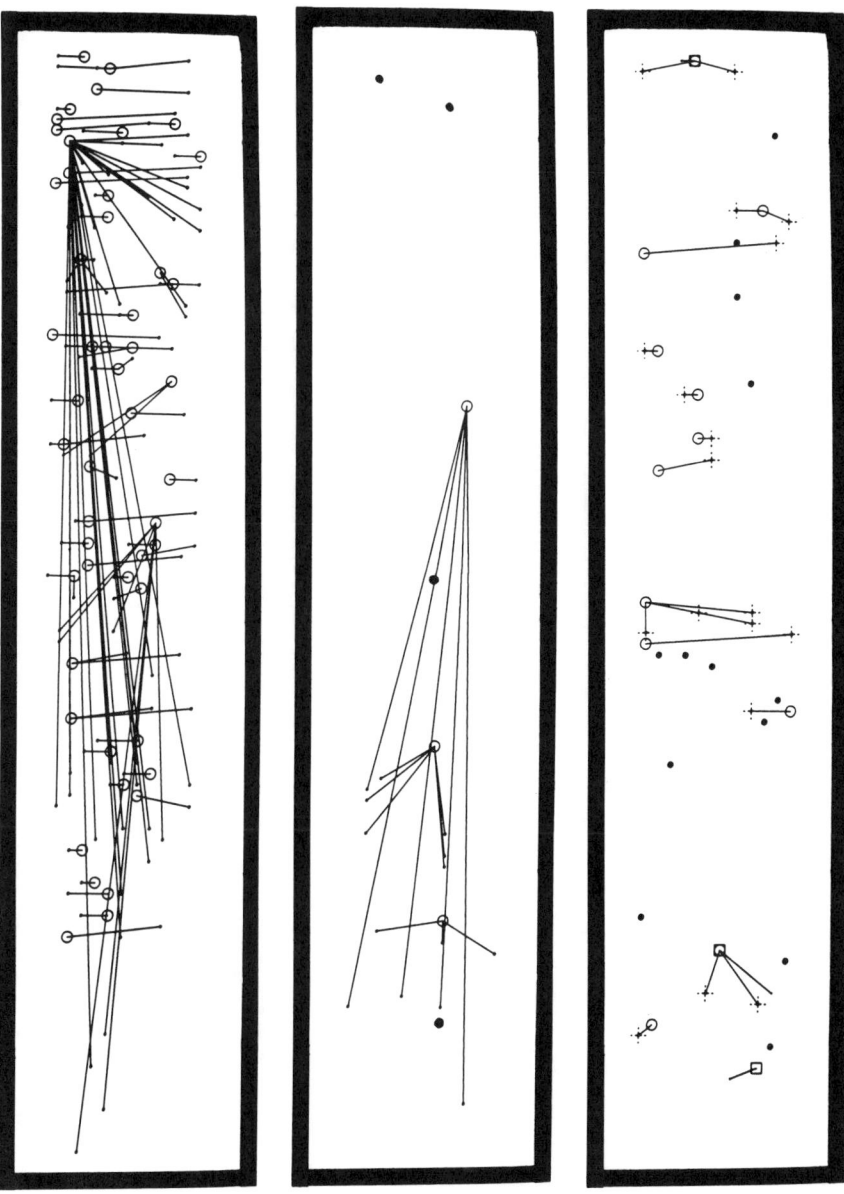

Figure 4.8. Friedman, "Why the American Economy is Depression Proof."

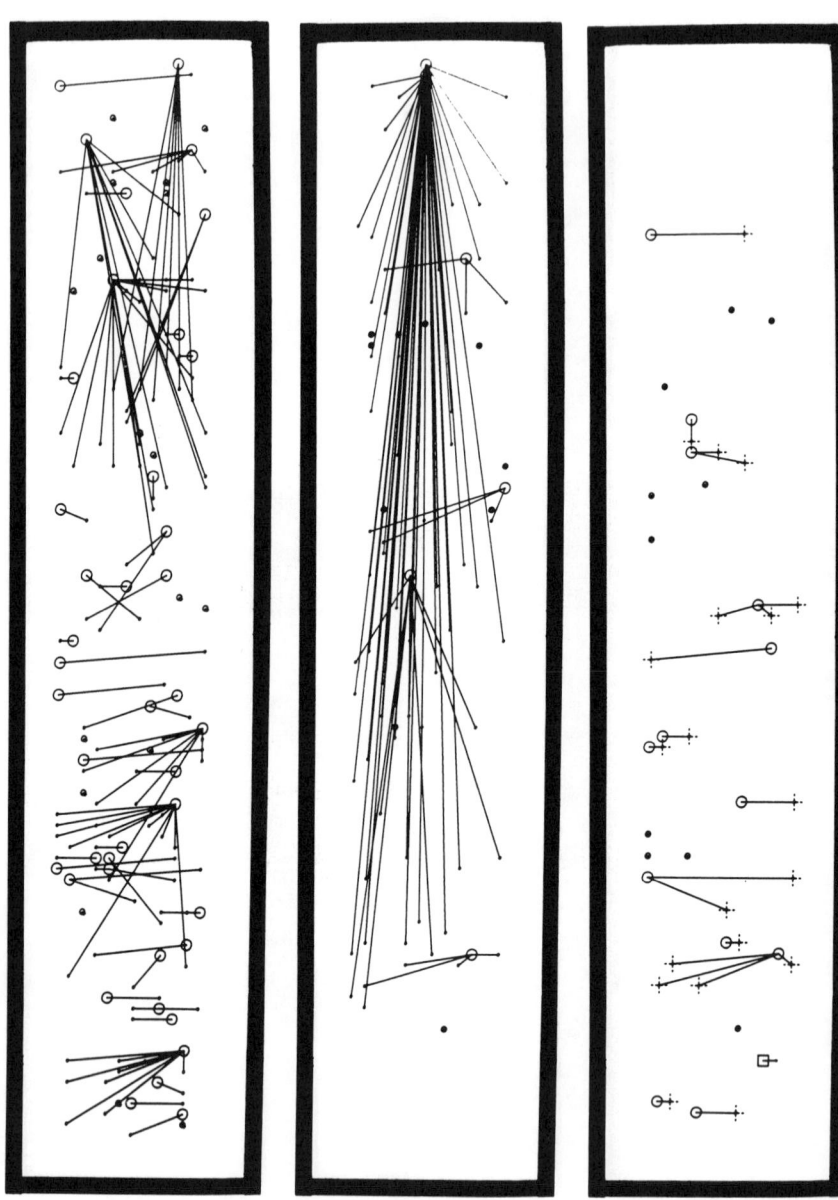

Figure 4.9. White, "Once More to the Lake."

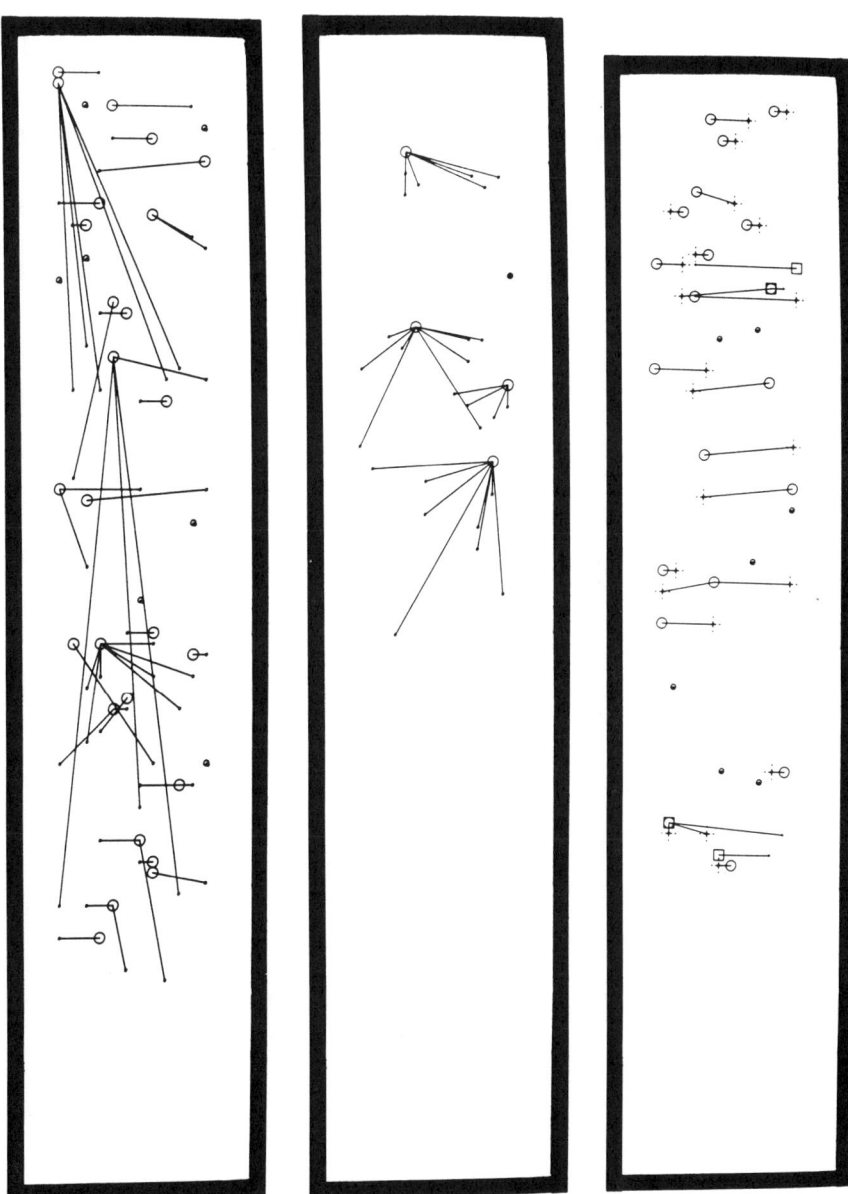

Definite Articles   Pronouns   Agent Displacement
Figure 4.10. Milford 1, *Zelda*.

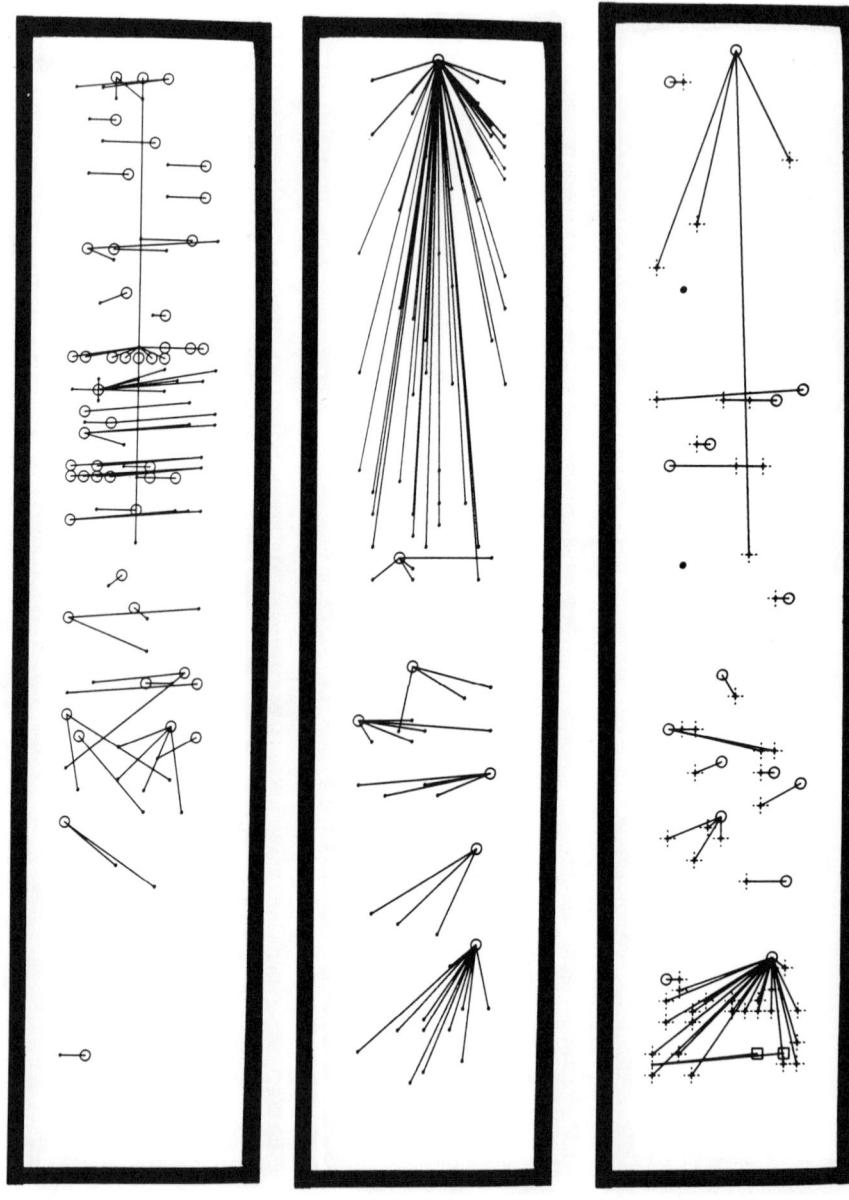

Figure 4.11. Sandburg 1, *Abraham Lincoln: The Prairie Years.*

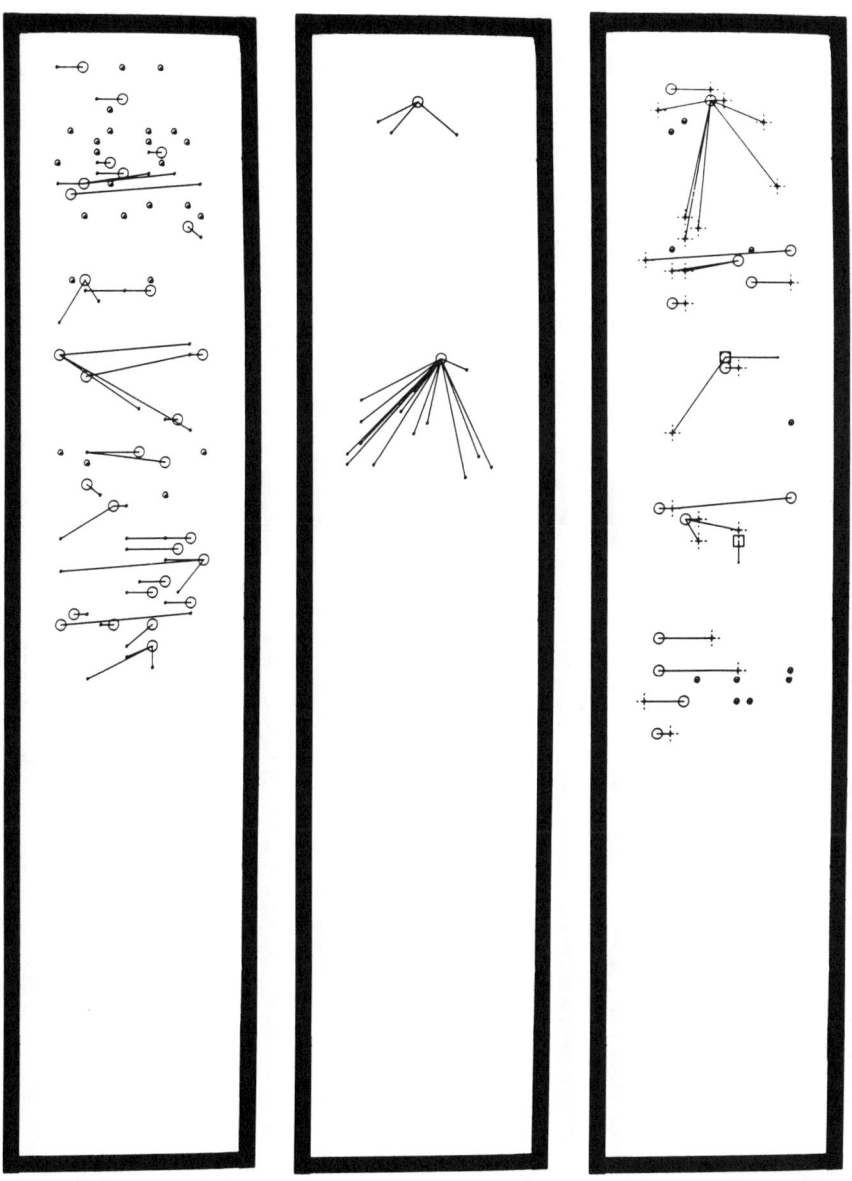

Definite Articles   Pronouns   Agent Displacement
Figure 4.12. Sandburg 2, *Abraham Lincoln: The Prairie Years.*

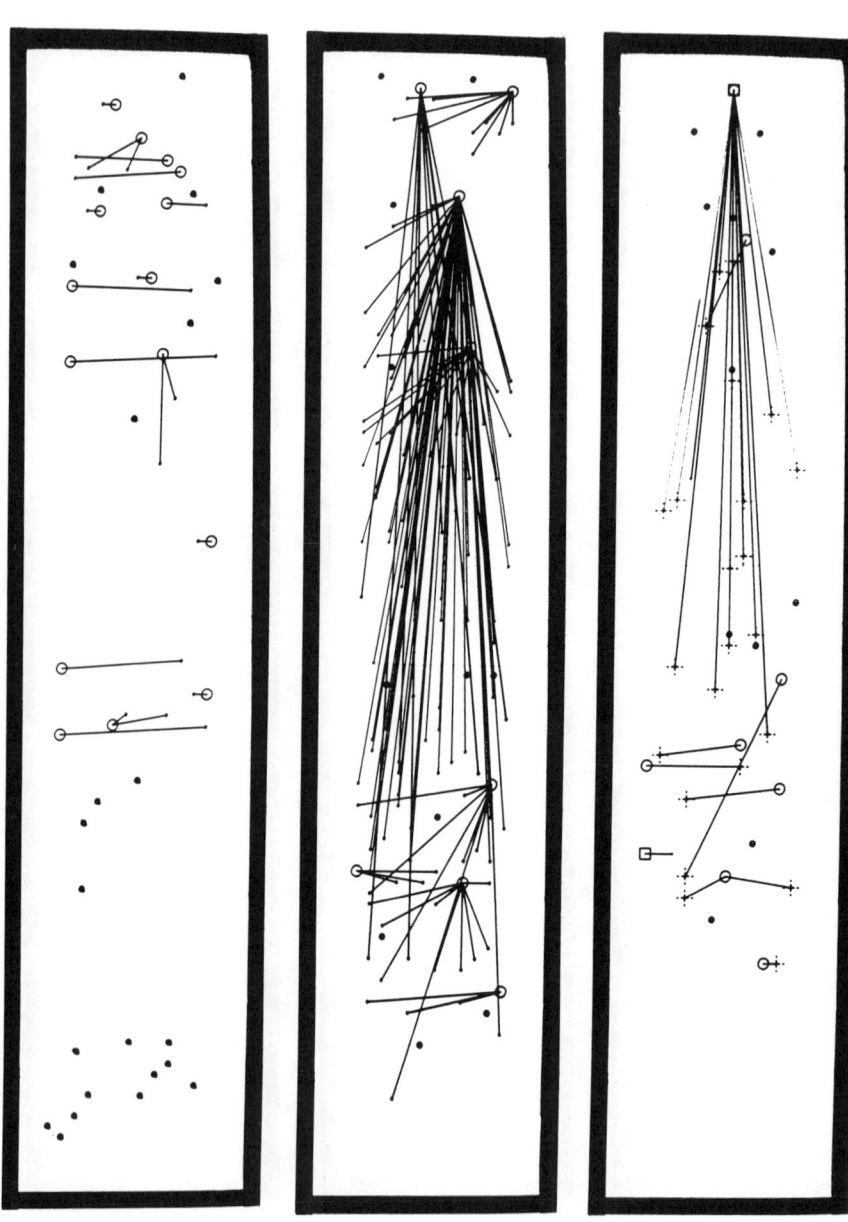

Figure 4.13. Clark 2, *The Ox-Bow Incident*.

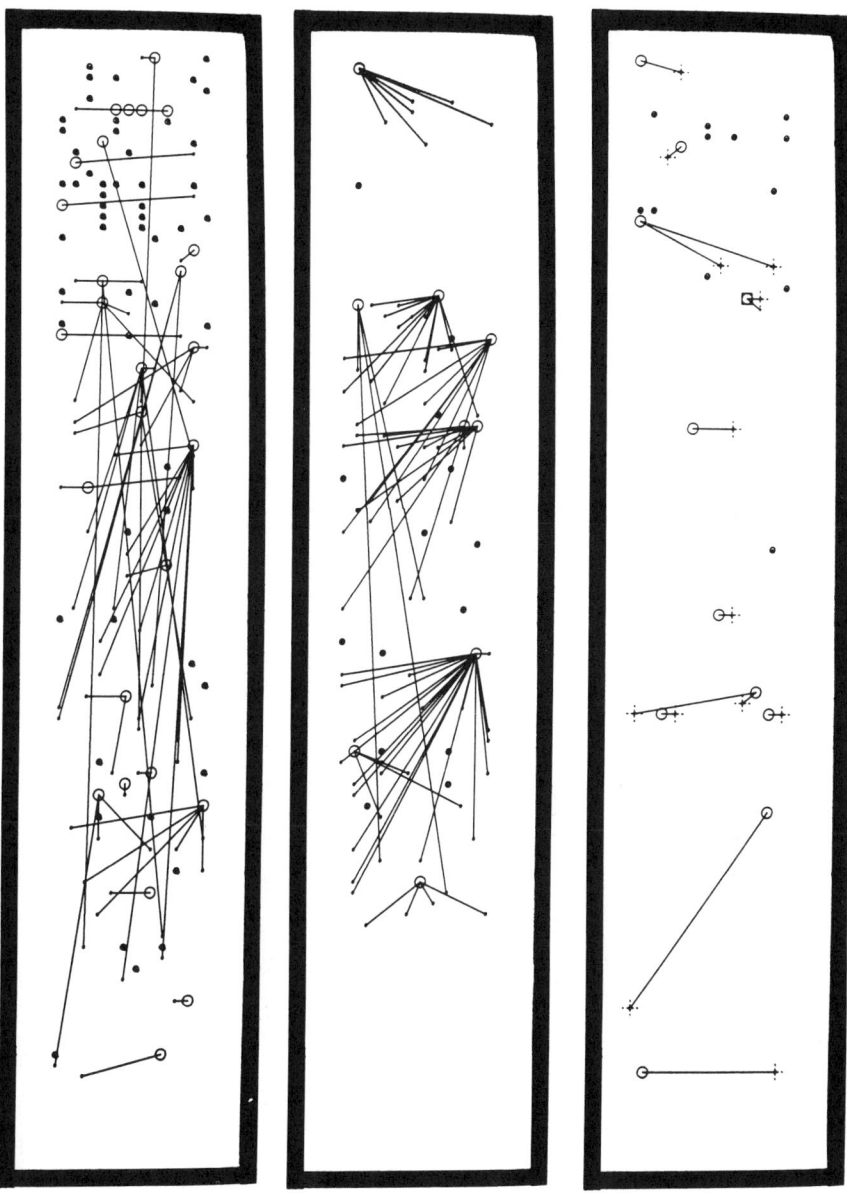

Definite Articles   Pronouns   Agent Displacement
Figure 4.14. Hemingway 1, *For Whom the Bell Tolls*.

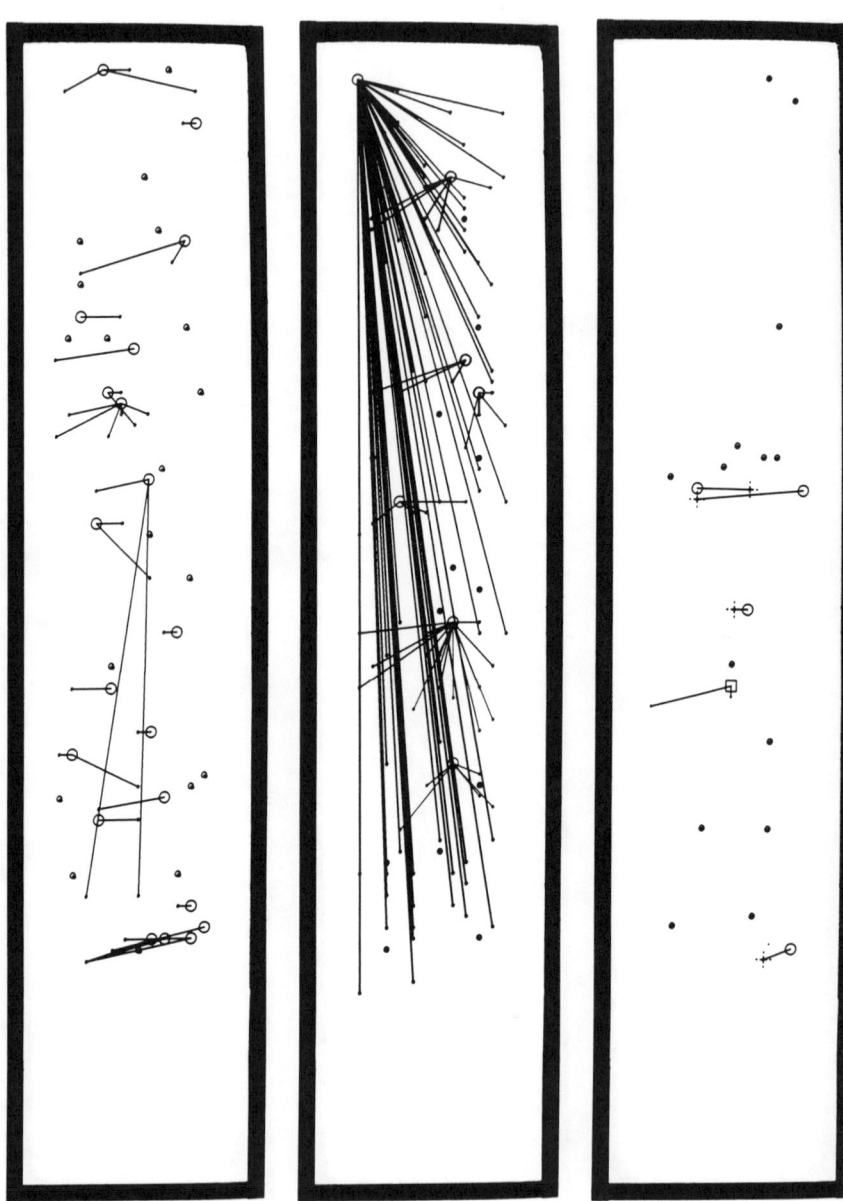

Figure 4.15. Hemingway 2, *For Whom the Bell Tolls.*

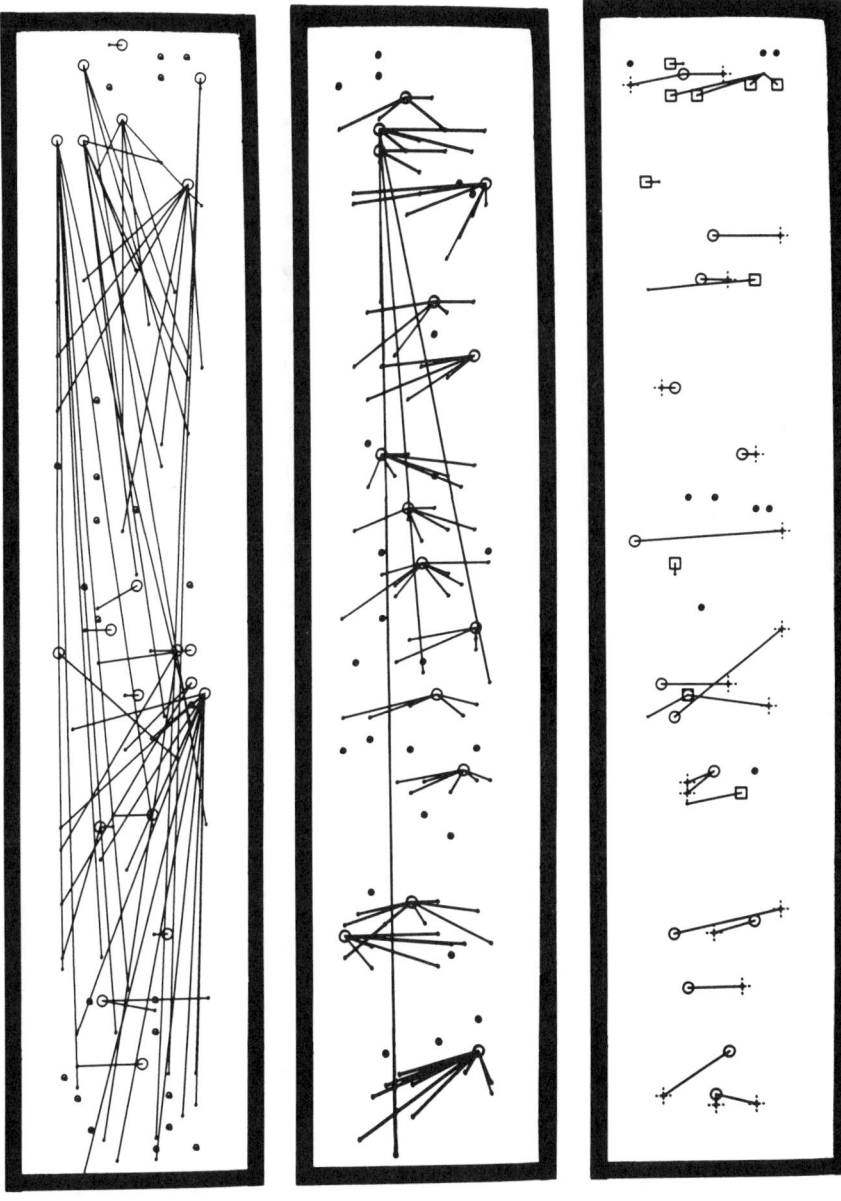

Definite Articles   Pronouns   Agent Displacement
Figure 4.16. Faulkner, "Dry September."

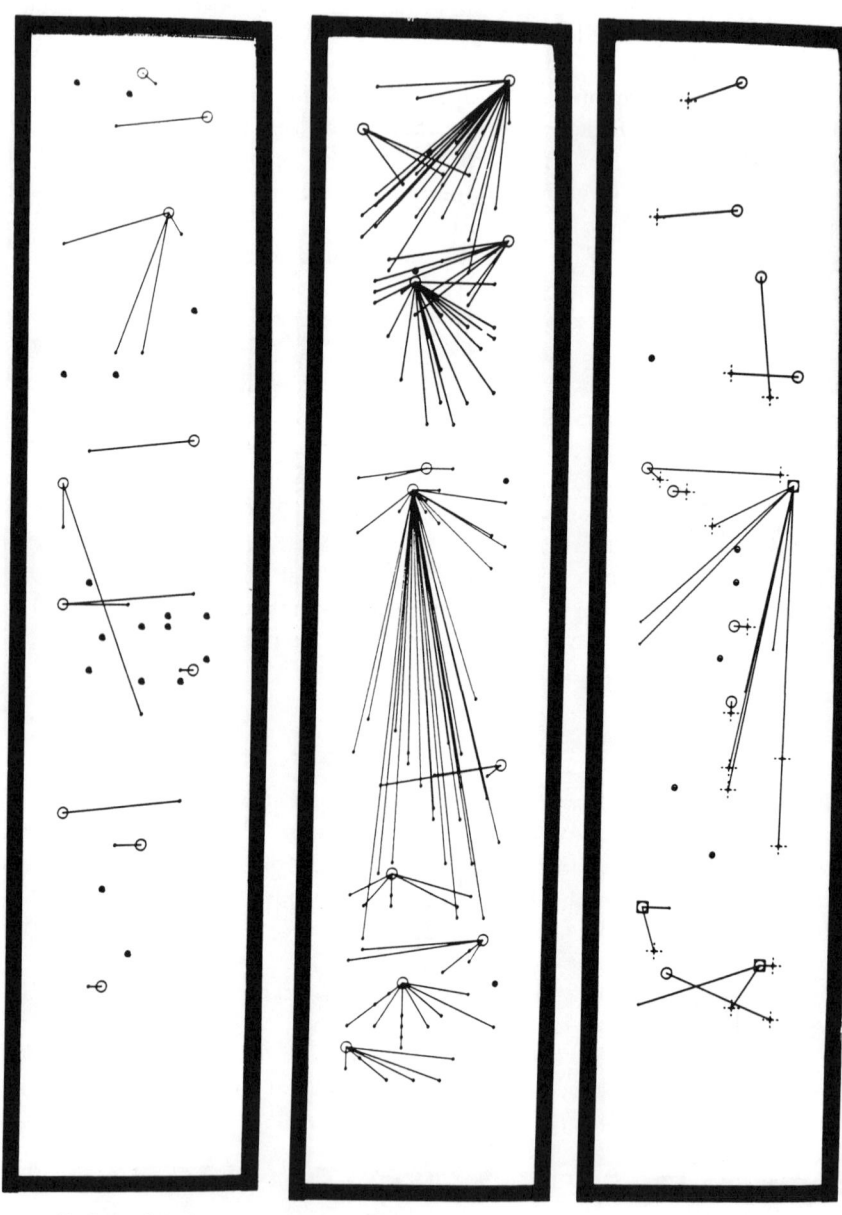

Figure 4.17. Porter, "The Jilting of Granny Weatherall."

distance and frequency for the mapped segments are reported in Tables P–T in Appendix B.

The left-hand map on each figure shows the pattern created by the definite article cohesive elements, the center map shows that for pronouns, and the right-hand map shows that for both kinds of agent displacements. The star-burst effect varies with the number of ties attached to one node. While it might seem that there is some significance in "left-skewed" or "right-skewed" or "centered" star-bursts, the seeming directional-orientation of these shapes is irrelevant. They are simply an accident of location.

A casual perusal of the sets of maps shows the pattern of each type of cohesion to be unique in each segment. On the one hand, this is surprising if we believe that there is an entity we call "text" which has characteristics common to all members of the class. We might expect more uniformity than is apparent in maps, especially within a text-type or even within a text. How much latitude can be allowed for the distinctive styles of individual writers to meet the definition of text is still unknown, but because of style, it appears to be possible to have wide variation within and between genres. Where variation is evident within a text, it would appear that the difference may have more to do with content than with style (a factor not dealt with in this study). However, until we know more about the relationship between form and content, the differences will be hard to account for.

Corroborating Numerical Data

The frequency of occurrence of the cohesive elements appears on the maps to vary considerably—from very dense to very sparse. The distances also vary, with some cohesive ties spanning nearly the whole passage, while others span minimal distances (i.e., with few or no intervening words). Indeed, it is difficult to examine the maps and not *sense intuitively* some of the generalities exhibited in the numerical data.

There are several perspectives from which we can examine the maps—by cohesion category, by text (for those with two segments presented), by text-type, by unfulfilled cohesion, and so on. This discussion is not intended to investigate all facets possible but rather to look at some of the possibilities and to see what kinds of questions need to be asked. Several observations can be made.

The first one is that, with exceptions such as Clark 2 (Figure 4.13), Sandburg 1 (Figure 4.11), and possibly Porter (Figure 4.17), the texts shown here make only minimal use of agent displacement to develop cohesion. This is not surprising in the light of the numerical data (Table 4.9) which shows the cohesion index for agent displacements in all text-types to be the lowest of the three categories. From these two kinds of evidence it seems that agent displacements are only peripherally fruitful as a cohesive device. The question arises, then, whether the exceptions—those texts that do use the potential cohesion of agent displacements—are idiosyncratic, or whether an analysis of a greater number of texts would show a greater range of agent displacement usage. If they are idiosyncratic, what do their writers gain or lose in choosing to use agent displacements? Are those writers that do make liberal use of them "better" than those that don't?

Another example shows how visual evaluation can be checked against the tables of data. While the map for Milford 1 (Figure 4.10) looks as if her use of agent displacement is minimal (because of the sparse pattern), in actuality the data show that her use is not unlike that of Clark 2 (Figure 4.13). That is, cohesive elements constitute 3.27 percent of the words in the text of Milford 1 according to Table M (Appendix B) while they constitute 3.26 percent in Clark 2, Table N. Furthermore, the number of unfulfilled cohesive elements—especially of passives—is very similar: Milford 1 has 63.64 percent unfulfilled passives with no unfulfilled -*ing* verbals while Clark 2 has 66.67 percent unfulfilled passives with 20.69 percent unfulfilled -*ing* verbals. From these figures, it would appear that Milford 1 should be the more cohesive (even if only by a small margin). However, the maps of the two text segments indicate that Clark 2 ought to be more cohesive as regards agent displacement. The difference appears to lie in the relative distances spanned by the networks and by the intersecting of networks (not accounted for in the numerical data). That is, where distances are small, there is less to hold a text together as the cohesion index factors illustrate (Tables P–T, Appendix B).

It is also apparent in the comparison of Clark 2 and Milford 1 that the average number of cohesive ties per node is greater in Clark 2 as the data confirm (Tables R and S). It stands to reason that, the more cohesion-terminals there are attached to a single node-frame, the more the mind is focused on that node, thereby creating greater cohesion.

Still another observation pertains to certain peculiarities that show up in the pronoun maps which can best be understood by looking at the numerical data. Two examples will suffice. One, White's personal essay (Figure 4.9), centers on the writer as speaker. In this case, where the first occurrence of a first person pronoun is marked as the node (as noted in Chapter 3), this one network spans almost the entire segment shown here, and in fact, would have extended farther if the segment had been longer. Interestingly, the percentage of words represented by the pronouns here (Table G) is very close to the median for all essay texts. It is, in fact, comparable to the two segments of Skinner (Table F). However the maps show quite clearly that a large proportion of cohesive elements in Skinner (Figure 4.6 and 4.7) are unfulfilled by the reader-subject while very few are unfulfilled in White's text. Furthermore, it is obvious in both the numerical data and on the maps that the cohesive networks in White span much larger chunks of physical text (319.40 for

White and 9.77 and 16.30 respectively for Skinner 1 and Skinner 2 as reported in Tables P and Q). It seems fair to say that White makes better use of pronoun cohesive elements.

The other example is that of the pronouns in the Hemingway text. The numerical data (Table I, Appendix B) for segment 1 and segment 2 are reasonably similar. The maps, in contrast, show a marked difference in the distances spanned by the networks. In the first segment (Figure 4.14), Hemingway speaks of Robert Jordan by his proper name several times, causing repeated reentry and little sustained distance. In the second segment (Figure 4.15), however, Jordan's proper name never appears. The node is present in the pages preceding the segment and in the following pages, but it is exophoric to this segment. The first instance of the Jordan-pronoun was designated as the node (as was the first pronoun in White's essay). That Jordan's name should be used so frequently in one segment and not at all in another is a curious thing. It might be partially explained by the fact that in the first passage, Jordan is interacting with another male character and so the pronouns would be confusing without the repeated reentry, but this does not account for Hemingway's choice to avoid reentry in the second passage. Such intriguing instances in the various texts need further consideration to understand why writers make the choices that they do.

One last observation is that there seems to be no pattern to the occurrences of unfulfilled cohesive elements which appear on the maps as single, unattached points, but it is plain that some occur in every text to a greater or lesser extent for every type of cohesion analyzed. Some of these might have been mitigated had Lakoff 1 and Skinner 1 (Figures 4.5 and 4.6, respectively), for instance, defined *we* thus giving it an intratextual node. However, the so-called editorial *we* is seldom defined in nonfiction, and so appears simply as a black dot representing an unfulfilled cohesive element. The number of such unfulfilled pronouns confirms the data shown in Tables F–J that for nonfiction the unfulfilled pronouns are over twice that of every other text-type. Whether writers of nonfiction *should* define pronouns is a different question.

A word of caution is in order regarding intuitive judgments made from map observation without checking relevant numerical data. In fact, such judgments may prove to be fallacious. This can happen because, without experience or training in evaluating what we see, our visual perception may be deceptive. Some examples will illustrate this problem.

At first glance, for instance, we might judge that the number of unfulfilled cohesive elements in Clark 2 (Figure 4.13) and in Hemingway 2 (Figure 4.15) to be about the same. The data belie this, however. Table D reports 25 percent more cohesive elements in Hemingway 2 than in Clark 2, but the percentage of unfulfilled cohesive elements to cohesive elements in Hemingway 2 is much lower (38 percent compared to 55 percent).

Likewise, the pronoun patterns (Figure 4.13 and 4.15) look very similar and appear to be equally cohesive (without taking into account the decision described in Note 33, Chapter 3). Again, the data indicate a greater differentiation than the eye sees. The cohesion index for Clark 2 is 1764.24 while the index for Hemingway 2 is 1098.39 (Table 4.7), the index for the Clark 2 text being over 50 percent larger than the Hemingway 2 text.

Another example compares the definite articles in Friedman (Figure 4.8), White (Figure 4.9), Hemingway 1 (Figure 4.14) and Faulkner (Figure 4.16). A visual study of this set would lead us to conclude that, except for differences in the number of unfulfilled cohesive elements, the cohesion should be about the same. Indeed, this turns out to be true for Friedman with a cohesion index of 263.78 (Table 4.5) and White with a cohesion index of 273.17 (Table 4.5). The cohesion index in the Hemingway 1 segment is a third larger than these two, however (cohesion index of 365.37 in Table 4.7). Perhaps most deceptive is the degree of difference shown by the Faulkner text which has a cohesion index of 783.93 (Table 4.8) which is more than twice that of Hemingway 1 and approaching three times that of Friedman and White. Since the averages of fulfilled cohesive elements per node are within a reasonable range are (Table Q, S, and T), it becomes obvious on reexamining the maps that the distances spanned in Faulkner are much greater than the other three and cause the notably greater cohesion index.

This is not to say that we cannot learn much from the maps alone; rather it suggests that without corroborating numerical data, our conclusions must be quite considered intuitive and tentative.

Observing Maps Without Relevant Numerical Data

There is abundant evidence that map observations allow us to coordinate our resulting intuitions with the known numerical data, but maps are also valuable for pointing out information that is not available in the statistics.

For one thing, the maps clearly show the intersections of networks—or absence of them.[16] However, without a very complex computer program, intersection cannot be measured numerically. Because of this, the research reported here does not deal with it further.

For another thing, we might expect a greater concentration of unfulfilled cohesion at the beginning of texts, particularly novels and short stories, where the writer is "setting the scene" (as described in Chapter 3). Even though the maps do not confirm this expectation the descriptive statistics used here cannot deal with this phenomenon at all.

A third observation is that the definite article patterns range from extremely complex (in about half the segments) to reasonably simple. The

---

[16] The maps might well have been constructed to show other kinds of information including reentry of nodes, but because of the difficulties of presentation and the sheer size of the task at hand, these factors were not included. In any case, by definition, a reentry network can never intersect with its primary entry network.

degree of complexity depends on the frequency of occurrence, the range of distances between cohesive elements and nodes, and the number of intersecting networks. (Perhaps reentry is a factor as well, but unfortunately, it is not accounted for.) For those texts that employ it, definite article cohesion would appear to be an extremely useful device for unifying a text. If this is so why don't all writers use it to the same extent? Is it simply a matter of a particular writer's style, or is it more related to subject matter?

Inferring the Complexity of Reader Processing

The maps of cohesion, separately or overlaid, show us only a tiny fraction of what our brains are working on when we read. At any given point in a physical text, our minds are making innumerable connections with what has gone before and predicting what will come. This is true not only for the three kinds of cohesion analyzed here, but also for every other type of text component. Our amazing grasp of grammatical concepts and textual properties allows us to work on many facets of text processing at one time.

Where the maps show cohesion patterns to be "dense" with much intersection, it is apparent that our minds are very busy. Busy-ness is not, however, equated with efficiency. Some of the density may be due to networks having many cohesive ties for one node so that the frame-node is well in mind and prediction is easy (as in White's essay). On the other hand, where the density is due to large numbers of unfulfilled cohesive elements (as in several of the map figures), the mind may be extra busy but the processing may be inefficient.

The maps of cohesion can only suggest the processing that is being carried on concurrently, but without the maps we have no other data that give us a holistic view of this complexity. Their importance, even in their present two-dimensional state, should not be underestimated, nor should their value to future examinations of the problem space "text."

Formulating the Rudiments of Texture

In Chapter 1, I suggested that text patterns such as those shown here are an integral component of texture in texts and that each text has a unique texture. Certainly the sets of maps shown in Figures 4.5–4.17 confirm this uniqueness. However we choose to portray this uniqueness,[17] it remains like a fingerprint of each text, but even the perception of this fingerprint will vary with each reader as the unique interpreter of that text. To better understand how a reader "reads" the texture of a text, we can learn from the maps generated here from location data.

---

[17] Barthes (1974), for instance, sees a text as a musical score which I find inadequate because a musical score by itself cannot show the multi dimensionality necessary to suggest texture.

In the building of a mental model of the writer's text, readers are, among other interpretive processes, creating cohesive ties. This means that, as they read sequentially (left to right, top to bottom in English), their minds are assimilating vast amounts of input data, among which connections must be made in order for them to judge a passage of writing to be "text." While readers are perceiving, processing, and interpreting definite noun phrases, they are, at the same time, also perceiving, processing, and interpreting pronouns, agent displacements and other text components which they encounter in the linear text. According to Minsky's frame postulates (1975), readers integrate information by first testing that information against previously established frames for identification, matching, or revision. For just these three types of cohesion, the processing is very complex; a holistic reading of a text multiplies that complexity exponentially.

Even though, at this time, we are not capable of describing all the mental operations necessary for readers to derive meaning from written texts, we do know that at any point in the text readers are involved in creating cohesive ties of one or more types. This processing can be suggested by "overlaying" the set of maps for one text. Figure 4.18 is an overlay of the maps from Faulkner's "Dry September" (shown in Figure 4.16). The varying shades of gray, from dark to light, depict the patterns of the definite article networks, the pronouns, and agent displacements respectively.

From the resulting composite patterns, it becomes abundantly clear that our minds are engaged in overwhelmingly complex operations as we read. At the same time, we sense how the patterns in a text accumulate to create texture. That is, when the maps are overlaid, some sections are more densely cohesive than others. The "surface" seems to vary three-dimensionally (as mountain peaks, high plateaus, and valleys vary) from the greatest density of networks to the least. Thus, the patterned occurrence of text structures when defined as a visual image is more palpable than might be imagined, and "texts" are certainly not flat, two-dimensional, nor even totally sequential. Indeed, they suggest textual synergism. Even so, it must be kept in mind that representing the mind's processing, the mind's perception of "text," in this fashion is simply a first attempt to illustrate a complex phenomenon which we are inadequately prepared to explain at this stage of our knowledge. Nevertheless, such overlaid maps tentatively confirm the third proposition addressed in this research, namely, that cohesion is a component of the texture of a text.

In summary, we can see that, without the occurrence statistics, the cohesion indexes, and the maps we could not verify the relative cohesiveness of text-types. These three measures of cohesiveness provide a tentative description of the operation of cohesion in written texts as perceived by a reader. Cohesiveness as a patterned component of texts is presented graphically by the maps, and its contribution to the texture of a text is suggested by an overlay of cohesive networks. The implications of these findings are explored in Chapter 5.

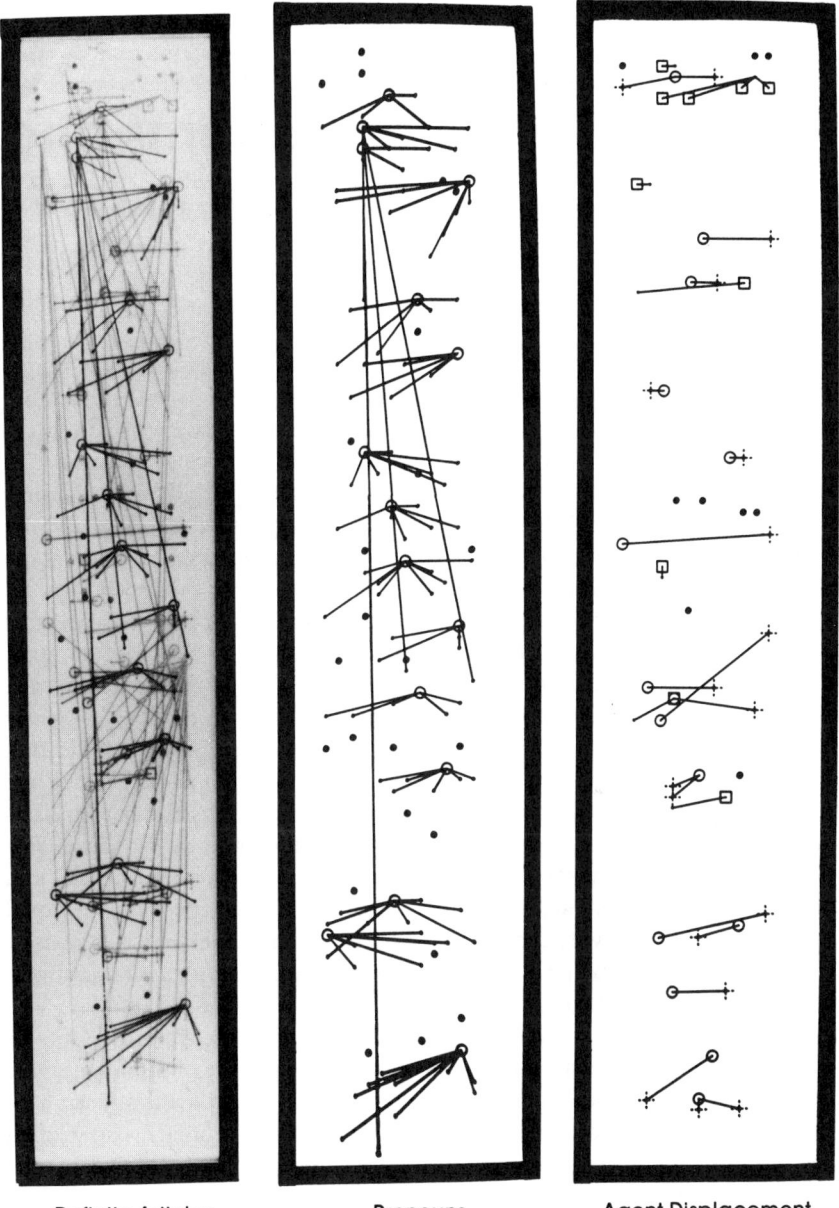

Definite Articles   Pronouns   Agent Displacement
Figure 4.18. Overlay of Cohesion Maps for Faulkner, "Dry September."

5
Cohesion Patterns and Texture in Texts

If textual synergism and the notion "text" could be explained by a simple truth, our predecessors would have no doubt done so long ago, but they are not simple concepts. Just as the sages of old had to discard their "plain facts" that the earth is flat and the sun revolves around it, so, too, may we have to discard our "simple truths" about the nature of text. Indeed, since Panini's Sanskrit grammar of 300 B.C., linguists have been forced to discard many theories of grammar as new "truths" have come to light. This means that the notion "text" may well be thought of quite differently in the future.

Many of the contemporary conventional parameters of text will likely be recategorized or even discarded and replaced by some as-yet-unthought-of organizing principle that better describes and explains the data of texts. Finding such a principle, however, will require that we be open to many kinds of thinking and will require us to acknowledge, as Lewis Thomas (1982) points out, that our conclusions are often ambiguous and tentative. Locking ourselves into set ways of thinking about texts disallows the possibility that the answers we seek lie outside of conventional wisdom. For example, thinking of texts as multidimensional, rather than sequential and linear, discourages easy answers, but it also frees us to view texts in novel ways. It suggests that we need to look at texts from new perspectives to cope with more complex text structures and to explain the complex interaction of form and meaning in texts.

Had past linguistic studies which concentrated on the minimal units of sound, or syntax, or semantics given us a definitive picture of these linguistic phenomena, there would perhaps be less need for such a reevaluation of textual truths. This is so even though it is likely that past scholars who studied the syntax of sentences probably considered their work as "global" compared to that of persons studying, say, Sanskrit aspirates. As our knowledge has expanded and minimal units have been put in larger perspectives, many of the earlier "truths" have already been revised or discarded as new questions have been raised and new "truths" have challenged the old.

Although it might seem that increasing the scope and depth of a study field would concomitantly increase the complexity of the problem under investigation, Minsky (1982, p. 2) says that the opposite is often true, that widening the scope often simplifies the problems at hand. This suggests that, if we had started studying texts by adequately defining the problem space, we might have eliminated much of the trial-and-error attendant to atomism. Nevertheless, until we find ways to describe a problem space holistically, we will be confined to discovering "complex truths about simple things" (Minsky, 1982, p. 5) which will need continual, and perhaps even drastic, revision as we gain additional insights into the holistic nature of the problem space. In the light of this problem, it will be useful to evaluate the approach and results of the research reported here.

EVALUATING THE METHODOLOGY

The Corpus

This preliminary investigation of patterns of cohesion as they relate to the texture of texts reflects the text-processing of one "real" reader (in the sense of Fillmore, 1982). No one would question the desirability of extending this kind of study to a larger group of readers. However, the extensive amount of time needed for a subject to mark 60,000 words of text segments suggests that carrying out the research with more than a few reader-subjects would probably require a change in the size of the database analyzed. The number of texts (35 in this case) or the number of text-types (5 here) or the length of the segments (800–1200 words) might be cut without impairing the validity of the findings. The question of what constitutes an appropriate database is one aspect of text studies that needs further investigation.

Because research in text processes depends on linguistic phenomena available in a physical text, the text data must be as "typical" as possible without being contrived for the purpose of illustrating a researcher's point. At present, there are no criteria for defining a typical text; however, choosing published and readily available texts partially circumvents this problem. It also provides a degree of attestation to the competence of the writers, but perhaps the same analysis of unpublished texts (i.e., in the main, by unskilled writers as in personal journals) would provide interesting comparative results.

The published texts analyzed here represent conventionally-accepted text-types, but certain types were not included (e.g., drama and poetry[1]). As suggested by the research results discussed in Chapter 4, conventional text-typing may be suitable for some kinds of analysis, but not necessarily all. For one thing, we lack standards for systematically classifying texts into groups

---

[1] Drama and poetry are special cases because neither is a conventional prose form overall.

which are mutually exclusive according to all possible criteria. Certainly literary scholars would argue with the simplistic scheme used here, but the scheme is one which is often used in college English departments; in fact, it is used without defining the criteria by which the categories are delimited, as far as I can determine. Still, literary scholars probably would not accept a shifting of text-types based solely on linguistic criteria even though it is obvious that, according to cohesion criteria, there is some question as to the validity of the five types examined here.[2] If we follow Minsky's suggestions (1975) about changing perspectives, we may find that an altogether different system for classifying texts is more appropriate than any currently in use.

In the meantime, the texts found to be "misfits" according to cohesion criteria may suggest other ways of looking at text-types. For instance, the content of Matthiessen's *The Snow Leopard* (a nonfiction account of a scientific data-gathering expedition in which he participated) is both journalistic and autobiographical. His extensive use of pronoun cohesion suggests that the book is more properly classified as biography if the frequency of occurrence of linguistic features is related to genre-assignment. Questions might also be raised about other texts which seem to "straddle" category lines, such as Sandoz's biography of her father, Angelou's autobiography, *The Autobiography of Malcolm X*, and personal essays. (See Appendix A.)

Another facet of the selection of specific texts for analysis has to do with the criterion of typicality which was mentioned above. Just which texts are "typical"? Is typicality an absolute amount or are there degrees of "typicalness"?[3] Is Steinbeck's *Grapes of Wrath* more typical than his "The Chrysanthemums"? Is Haley's *The Autobiography of Malcolm X* more typical than Sandoz' *Old Jules*? A strictly statistical approach to text selection would argue for a random selection of, say, every 100th book listed in *Books in Print* for every 10th year. No such guidelines were established in determining the particular texts to be included here other than designating the 20th century as a reasonable time period and writing in English by Americans as the cultural milieu. There are other questions. Are seven texts in each category enough? Is the 20th century too broad or too narrow to be significant? Should the corpus include different types of writing by the same author (e.g., a novel and an essay)?

While the corpus for this study included works such as nonfiction texts in several disciplines (including two textbooks), assorted essays, and a mixture of acclaimed and nonacclaimed fiction, they all met the criterion that they had

---

[2] A basic question, which I will not attempt to answer, is whether it is possible to define the parameters of "text" without the input of both linguists and literary scholars.

[3] In regard to typicality, text linguist-statisticians might profitably determine what length of text passage and how many texts must be analyzed to assure validity according to inferential statistics.

been deemed worthy of being published. None of them defied ordinary writing conventions in any significant way, and in this sense, they can be said to be typical. However, there are works of literature that do defy writing conventions for the purpose of foregrounding certain ideas or certain characters. These works, like poetry and drama, present a confounding factor which was deliberately ignored for this preliminary exploration, but must eventually be dealt with.

The method of selecting texts adopted here is justified by the tentative nature of the research in finding pertinent and promising questions for further study. This does not mean that, because the texts were not chosen according to statistical randomness, the results are less interesting or less valid. They may or may not be, but the question of selecting an appropriate corpus from among the myriad physical texts available remains problematic.

It would be possible, of course, to concentrate a study of the notion "text" by limiting the study to just one genre, or just one text, or even just one kind of cohesion, but such a study would continue the atomism of the past without learning much about the problem space itself. Even the limited scope of this study is a compromise between what is humanly possible to process and analyze and what is most useful. Eventually we must find generalities from a broad spectrum of text components in a broad spectrum of texts with a broad spectrum of readers to fully understand how texture is realized.

The Use of Computers

This research on cohesion as a component of texture in texts greatly extends the length of text passages analyzed and increases the number of texts examined, but still more data will need to be analyzed to gain an adequate picture of the problem space "text." The computer has, of course, made it possible to envision a systematic and complete analysis of text processing. Scanners which can read printed pages into computer memories will save endless amounts of time for text researchers who must now either type in every text or be limited to only those texts that have already been entered (such as the Brown University Corpus). Even so, in spite of the increasing sophistication of computers and computer users, humans are still responsible for many of the operations that computers are not yet smart enough to do.[4]

The potential for combining multidimensional graphics and printed text on the computer allows for possibilities that have barely been tapped so far. Ultimately the task of text analysis will be simpler and faster as computers become even faster, more powerful and more sophisticated and we become

---

[4] Although we have progressed mightily from the time when monks spent their lifetimes painstakingly copying manuscripts—and even from the advent of the printing press—unfortunately, reader-subjects still have to do much of the "handwork" of text-marking.

more imaginative in using them to serve our purposes. Cohesion is reasonably amenable to analysis of linear-based elements, but more complex linguistic expressions (e.g., linguistic expressions that have been subjected to certain kinds of transformations, such as question formation and embedded clauses) will require more imaginative methods of text analysis.

Though this study looked at only one subset of one text component, cohesion,the SNOBOL4 AND PL1-FORTRAN computer programs are flexible enough to be adapted for analysis of other types of syntax-related text components. The computer programs described in Chapter 3 fulfill the needs of this research well. The major task is the marking of nodes and elements to done by humans. Once completed (by either a subject or a researcher entering the data into the computer), the calculations are carried out almost automatically. Thus, additional statistical testing would be appropriate for a larger group of subjects.

The Working Definitions

Research design, however it is carefully planned to produce and interpret the data, is irrelevant if adequate delimiting and defining terms are not spelled out, a problem often neglected in discourse studies. Two major definitions circumscribe this study: text and cohesion. The first, text, is defined as the mental model constructed by a reader using as input data a physical text (which is the representation of the mental model constructed by a writer.) This characterization, which allows for reader idiosyncracy, is the only one possible—given, on the one hand, the inaccessibility of the writer's mental model and, on the other, the fact that textual synergism is dependent on reader interpretation.

Cohesion is also a mental construct resulting from reader-processing; it is a textual component. Readers, on encountering lexical expressions with explicit or implicit syntactic signals for cohesion (cohesive elements), attempt to associate and most often complete an association (cohesive tie) between the element and another lexical expression by which it is identified (node). The node may be intratextual or inferred by the reader from extratextual information. Texture appears to be rather more palpable than heretofore shown because reader-processing of cohesion is accessible for suggesting how the texture of a text is created.

The definitions of definite article cohesion, pronoun cohesion, and agent displacement cohesion have worked well for this research, but, as suggested in Chapter 3, they are not without problems. Although some future recategorization may prove to be more adequately descriptive, for a first attempt at exploring their roles in creating texture, these definitions are satisfactory.

On the basis of the results discussed in Chapter 4, these definitions are reasonable and there seems to be no reason to modify them at this time.

EVALUATING TEXT AS PROCESS

One of the underlying premises of this research says that any study of text must be concerned with "text as process." This premise recognizes that explaining textual synergism requires that we first understand how readers interpret physical texts produced by writers. Not all readers have the same mental capability or training or world knowledge. This means that their processing and the results of that processing vary and, therefore, the "synergistic sum" of any given text also varies to some degree among a given set of readers. Learning just how much uniformity and variation actually exists as readers process texts will greatly enhance our understanding of textual synergism and the definition of the problem space "text."

Textual synergism is no doubt influenced by the contribution of the writer's input to the reader, but it is difficult to test this supposition for reasons stated earlier. The fact that a single writer produces a particular written text (while any number of readers may process that text) makes statistical validation of this input even more difficult. We are left to speculate about what direct or indirect effect a writer's input has on readers' interpretations. Nevertheless, a physical text contains, in a sense, the artifacts of a writer's creative input.

Writer-Induced Potential for Cohesion

Many aspects of writers writing and readers processing cohesion networks are suggested by this study, but not all of them are addressed in the research design and implementation. Even so, the results support our intuitions that these speculations are nontrivial and worth pursuing in the future. For one thing, it is probably not unrealistic to say that writers, by and large, have little awareness of their use of cohesion—except to make sure that pronouns agree with their nodes in person and number and to decide which article, if any, is needed with a particular noun. Still, physical texts, the result of stylistic choices, can affect the way a reader processes them.

For one thing, if cohesive elements permeate a text, we would expect that readers will perceive a written text to be cohesive, as held together by the various components of which it is constituted. If cohesive elements are sparse and/or ambiguous, we could predict that a reader's processing should increase in difficulty; if the potential of interpretable cohesive elements is large, the reader's processing should decrease in difficulty. Therefore, the sheer number of cohesive elements a writer makes available to readers will influence their ease of interpretation.

If, however, a writer chooses to simply repeat nodes without using many cohesive elements, we might expect that readers would find the content equally cohesive (but probably boring for its repetitiveness). Our intuition and knowledge of the construction of physical texts tells us that we would expect there to be a relationship between the phenomenon of node repetition and memory retention. It is not, however, accounted for in this research (discussed in Chapter 4), nor is it discussed as a possible factor in retention in Gentner's study (1981).

It seems likely that, if a writer selects one type of syntactically marked cohesive element rather than another (e.g., a pronoun instead of an epithet or a noun phrase with a definite article), this choice may also influence a reader's success or failure in perceiving a cohesive tie. This can happen because the number of semantic connections to the node represented by each option may vary, as the Connectivity Hypothesis (Gentner, 1981) suggests. Furthermore, the Theory of Anaphoric Hierarchy suggests, if a particular choice is much less specific than another, readers may be less likely to make an appropriate association between an element and its node.

While Gentner (1981) does not suggest that distance influences a subject's memory for a node, it is certainly a logical extension of her theory. In order for a text which is longer than a few sentences to be perceived as a unified whole, it must have some cohesive components with the power to extend beyond paragraph boundaries. In other words, a writer must somehow make the potential for connections possible across chunks of text in order for a reader to judge a text to be unified. While every kind of cohesive device available in English may appear in a text, not all meet this distance criterion. For instance, adjective clauses are a cohesive device, but if writers position them too far from the nouns they modify, readers may be confused about which node is appropriate, if any (e.g., dangling modifiers). The decision by a writer to separate a node from its various elements can enhance the unity of a text even with intervening text—if the semantic connections between an element and its node are clear and "sufficient" (an undefined amount). The three types of cohesion analyzed in this research—pronouns, definite articles, and agent displacements—show that some writers are better than others in using this distance factor, but all of them extend cohesive ties across sentence and paragraph boundaries (Chapter 4).

Both the Frame Theory and the Connectivity Hypothesis allow us the freedom to posit some kind of a multidimensional knowledge store based on semantic connections. If we accept that our knowledge is organized in the mind in other than fixed memory bins accessed linearly and that our understanding of text is neither rigid nor static, the notion that cohesion operates cataphorically as well as anaphorically is perfectly reasonable. Since, as Stoddard (1981) points out, cataphoric pronoun cohesive elements are very rare, the position of these cohesive elements is relatively insignificant as far as a writer's stylistic choices are concerned. Still, cataphoric cohesion can be an advantage to a writer in allowing variation in word order which may have the effect of foregrounding information.

It might appear on the surface that the intersection of two or more cohesive networks would be confusing to readers in interpreting cohesive ties. This could, of course, be the case if a writer has not clarified male/female pronouns carefully. For instance, if the networks for two named men intersect, it can be confusing as to which male pronoun belongs to which man. Where the genders are different, there should be no problem. Writing which involves very much intersection of cohesion networks is a challenge for the reader. Still, the complexity of intersection (as shown in the maps, Figures 5-18) probably does not adversely affect the reading of competent readers.

Reader-Supplied Cohesion

Once a writer has marked cohesive elements syntactically, the situation becomes a bit like the proverbial question as to whether a tree falls in the forest if no one is present to hear it. If no reader acts on the writer's clues, does cohesion exist? It does, presumably, exist for the writer who causes the placement of cohesive elements in the written text, but if readers cannot hear the tree—cannot create cohesive ties—then we would have to question whether cohesion truly exists. The numerical data generated by the reader-subject in this study confirms that in every work examined, for every type of cohesion, there are cohesive elements with appropriate, explicit nodes and, negatively, there are some cohesive elements without appropriate nodes and the former far outweigh the latter.[5] From this evidence, it seems clear that writers create potential for cohesion even though some cohesive elements remain unfulfilled.

This means that, if readers have appropriate frames already established for the concepts referred to in the written text, or are able to establish them, they should be able to create cohesive ties most of the time. The organization of knowledge in the mind not only allows, but perhaps encourages, the seeking out of cohesive ties to make sense out of what is read.

On the other hand, if readers have not established or cannot establish appropriate knowledge frames, what happens to their reading? Are there different levels of frustration that set in which, perhaps, vary with the degree of specificity indicated by the writer's choice of cohesive elements (as suggested by Lakoff, 1976) or, perhaps, with the degree of importance the reader assigns to it? Further, are there situations where readers are effectively stopped in their reading because their knowledge frames—or memories—fail and they cannot make connections? How much and what kinds of failure will readers tolerate? These problems relate directly to the reading process, but

---

[5] These statistics are discussed in detail in Chapter 4. Tables 4.1-4.3 in Chapter 4 and Tables A-O in Appendix B report the numerical data.

also to the notion of "readability" of texts, and deserve an answer before we understand what "text" is all about.

The problem of failing to process cohesive ties might seem to be greater with ties stretching over large chunks of texts. However, in such cases (as, for instance, in Faulkners's "Dry September"), failure may be more related to memory than to a lack of knowledge frames. Where stories introduce many characters at once, causing considerable intersection (as in some Russian novels), the mind may be sorely put to hold all the nodes until they begin to sort themselves out. This problem might also be true in texts that deal with subjects quite foreign to their readers, such as textbooks in linguistics or physics for college freshmen with no background in the subject.

The second hypothesis for this research states that the relative cohesiveness of texts concerns the nature of the patterns created by cohesion networks (i.e., the number of ties per node and the relative distance between the ends of the ties). If one text appears numerically to be more cohesive than another, as the results discussed in Chapter 4 indicate, do readers perceive this to be true? Is the Connectivity Hypothesis valid at a larger scale, perhaps? That is, will a greater number of cohesive ties overall in a text make the text more memorable? These are interesting questions whose answers, if they turn out to be "yes," will further affirm the second hypothesis and the efficacy of the Connectivity Hypothesis.

Certainly, cohesive ties that span sentence and paragraph boundaries have greater potential for unifying a text and making it more cohesive. Referring again to Faulkner's "Dry September" (Figure 4.16), several men are introduced in short conversational paragraphs reducing the average number of pronoun cohesive elements per node and the average distances per fulfilled cohesive element.[6] In contrast, Miss Minnie Cooper is referred to by name early in the segment and thereafter is always referred to by a pronoun. While there are few references to her in the early part of the story, she is the only female and so the ties that extend the length of the segment are not confusing. The effect of this strategy is to emphasize her role while pulling the text together. Cohesive ties across large spans of text are potentially risky for a writer, but the rewards for their effective use are probably worth it.

EVALUATING THE RESULTS

Numerical Data

Using numerical data to prove a point is a common form of argument. The numerical results in this study, while extensive, do not exhaust the potential

---

[6] This is also apparent in the pronoun maps, Figures 4.9 and 4.14.

for the three types of cohesion analyzed here (i.e., definite articles, pronouns, and agent displacements), let alone the numerous other kinds of cohesion (see Halliday & Hasan, 1976). Additional data accounting for intersection and reentry would add another dimension to the results. Data accounting for definite noun phrases without the definite article marking (e.g., "Voters who. . .") would perhaps be interesting and useful. Data describing the semantic relationship between passive verbs and -*ed* and -*ing* verbals and their nodes would help us to understand Gentner's Connectivity Hypothesis (1981). Nevertheless, the data gathered here provides valuable insights into the ubiquitousness of, the power of distance in, and the relative cohesiveness of three kinds of cohesive devices.

Visual Models of Cohesion and Texture

Patterns in texts rarely insinuate themselves into our consciousness, except, perhaps, in the case of well-written parallel structures where repetition of form and resulting rhythm cannot be ignored (as in Lincoln's well-known quote "of the people, by the people, and for the people"). Nevertheless, most readers, if asked, could probably identify some patterns such as the SVO (subject-verb-object) word order in English. Certainly, their existence in written texts has been long recognized by linguists. Although these patterns can be and are systematically described, they rarely are depicted in a visual form.[7]

Visualizations can be useful because most people have a strong visual orientation. We remember more readily if we have information in print or in graphic form than if we simply receive it aurally. This is particularly evident, for instance, when people older than teenagers, say, try to learn a new language. Furthermore, it is often easier to perceive relationships through graphics than through written words. A graphic model of knowledge frames and the notion of connectivity and cohesion may give us a better understanding of how these relate to language functions in our brains. The three maps for each text segment in this study add to that understanding by suggesting the complexity of language processing. In addition, the overlay map Figure 4.18) provides compelling evidence for both the simultaneous processing of cohesive ties by readers and for their perception of the rudiments of texture.

The maps of cohesion, computer-generated from word-location data (Figure 4.5-4.17), are useful to confirm visually our intuitions and the numerical data in this study. We can readily see that those texts spanned most

---

[7] I suggest that Grimes' Thurman charts (1975), Barthes' musical score (1974), Gutwinski's tables (1976), and Collins, Brown, and Larkin's staging model (1980) are examples of previous attempts.

comprehensively by many cohesion networks having multiple cohesive elements are the most unified—at least as regards pronouns, definite noun phrases, and agent displacements.

Furthermore, the maps show how networks consisting of many ties focus attention on the nodes of these networks, thereby giving rhetorical emphasis to that node through syntactic marking. It might even be possible to trace major or minor characters through networks of pronouns and epithets and to trace major or minor themes through networks of definite articles. The relationship between form and content seems to become tangible with this visual aid.

Still, the question of texture remains. In Chapter 1, I suggested that texture exists because texts (as differentiated from physical texts) are not merely linear and sequential but are multidimensional. If we could map every type of text component, including form, content, stylistic and rhetorical components, and could overlay the patterns which emerge, we would have many layers constituting the base from which the "bas relief" of texture would become apparent. Thus, I would claim that, when literary scholars speak of a writer reintroducing this character or that at this point or that to advance the plot,[8] the resulting pattern would coincide with the cohesion patterns that flesh out the texture. The result of our perceptions of this texture may well have to do with what scholars mean when they say that a certain writer "does not have much depth" or that another writer's ideas are "rich and colorful." The nature of texture at this stage must remain speculative, but the maps of cohesion provide rudimentary evidence for its existence.

IMPLICATIONS OF COHESION AND TEXTURE IN TEXTS

Since it seems certain from the data and the maps that cohesion and texture are components of every text, how does their presence affect the producers and processors of those texts? It is important to look further into the processing involved. For instance, what does a writer gain from using cohesive devices, and does it matter whether a reader finds a text cohesive or not? If it does matter, it is logical to assume that so-called "good" writers will maximize a reader's chances of recreating the writer's mental text. This would mean that writers who are sensitive to their readers would aim to minimize the number of possible interpretations (taking into account particular target audiences addressed by writers). If this is true, is maximizing the perception of cohesion crucial to achieving interpretability?[9] Or stated otherwise, how much unfulfilled cohesion will hinder interpretability?

---

[8] This would also be true in nonfiction when writers introduce this theme or that.

[9] There are many other questions about the relationship of cohesion and readability to be

Cohesion serves several rhetorical functions. The major function, of course, is to give unity to a text. In order to write a coherent text, writers must use every device possible to create both intratextual and contextual unity. We have already seen how cohesion nodes having multiple cohesive elements and how cohesive ties spanning varying lengths of text accomplish this (Chapter 4).

Cohesive ties also provide patterned predictability which fulfills reader expectation. They are as predictable in English as, say, noun-verb number agreement. If readers are to have reasonable expectations of what they will encounter in a text—as regards cohesion structures, writers must meet those expectations in the way they write. If they do, readers will probably be able to process a text with reasonable efficiency. If they don't (and certainly some freshman compositions show that not all writers do), readers will be confused. This means that readers do not have to do a memory search each time a pronoun cohesive element attached to a common node appears, as long as consistency is maintained. In White's personal essay, "Once More to the Lake" (Figure 4.9), for instance, readers count on the node for the pronoun *I* to be consistent throughout. If White's use of the first person singular were not consistent, readers would have to work hard to make sense of the writing.

Cohesion functions to reduce some kinds of redundancy.[10] As was suggested earlier, if every mention of a person or a theme were expressed the same way, the text would become very redundant, not to mention boring. Pronouns, epithets with definite articles, and displaced or deleted agents allow variation.

In spite of these admirable functions, the data in this study show that published writers do not spell everything out for the reader. In fact, several rhetorical strategies can be made more effective through unfulfilled cohesion. One strategy is the creative use of inferential gaps which allow a writer to circumscribe a target audience by excluding those readers who do not have appropriate frames and thus cannot make appropriate connections—while the intended readers have no problems with interpretation.[11]

A second strategy is at work when writers of fiction (especially short

---

answered as well, such as the effect of intersection on readers' perceptions and the effect of texture on reading efficiency.

[10] Stylistic options, such as agent displacements, are a case in point. Redundancy is reduced because this category of cohesion necessarily involves some kind of deletion (of the agent-node or an auxiliary verb as well as the preposition *by*). In other words, a writer could choose to retain or delete an agent-node in a passive structure depending on whether it would be helpful to reduce redundancy or not.

[11] For instance, a university freshman reading Skinner's *Beyond Freedom and Dignity* may not have enough knowledge to complete even the bridges that are available, let alone those which must be inferred. Whether this effect would be due to Skinner's misunderstanding his audience or to his deliberate desire to thus limit his audience is unknown.

stories) use a definite article noun phrase at the beginning of a story without a previous node. They are willing to risk a reader's being momentarily confused to emphasize the immediacy of the narrative event. The texts by Faulkner, Clark, and Lee are examples of this.

A third strategy for using unfulfilled cohesion makes use of deliberate ambiguity. The effect of this is to intrigue those readers who enjoy finding alternate interpretations. Writers can create depth in their writing by the effective use of ambiguity. Cohesion ambiguity can also be used to mislead an audience, as is often done in propaganda. This is particularly common with pronouns such as the editorial *we* and agent displacements, especially the passives.[12]

What are the risks for a writer in choosing to use cohesive elements—either fulfillable or not? I would suggest that a writer who is too specific, who spells out too much, may talk down to the reader, may be repetitive, or may appear unimaginative. The writer who is not specific enough or allows for too much ambiguity risks misinterpretation by readers. It is clear that writers must and do take risks in balancing fulfilled and unfulfilled cohesion in order to achieve their rhetorical goals. Whether writers who have learned how to take these risks and still achieve maximum clarity thereby produce critically acclaimed writing is yet another unanswered question.[13]

It is not easy to separate the strategies of the writer from the strategies of the reader because they play on each other. There are several aspects of the interpretive process that bear looking into.

In the reading process, readers constantly must fit the input data into their individual knowledge frames. This operation is so instantaneous that we are hardly aware of doing so, especially when old information fits the default frame terminal without adjustment. Only when new information demands the creation of a new frame or a change of default value, are we likely to become aware of making such adjustments. If we fail to find an appropriate node or create a wrong frame node or make a wrong inference, our reading may be effectively disrupted or we may have to adjust our perceptions later.[14] Such an adjustment may, in fact, account for being "led down the garden

---

[12] For instance, in Skinner 2, he writes: *We are told* that what *is threatened* is 'man qua man,' or 'man in his humanity'... These are not very helpful expressions, but they supply a clue. What *is being abolished* is autonomous man..." (Emphasis added). *(Beyond Freedom and Dignity)*

Without the agents for these passive verbs, we cannot rely on their authenticity. Useful discussions of the motivation for such unfulfilled passives are found in Stanley's work (1975, 1978).

[13] A tangential question is whether critically acknowledged writing is necessarily high in readability.

[14] Such instances of adjustment are not uncommon in reading. A personal example will illustrate. The first sentence, in O'Connor's story, reads, *The grandmother didn't want to go to Florida.* "The grandmother" image in my mind triggered an association with a sweet, plump little woman—an image that had to be altered considerably a few sentences later.

path" as we sometimes are (e.g., when a murder mystery writer tricks us into inferring that the butler did it).

Fillmore (1982) attempts to deal with one aspect of these complexities by positing an "ideal" vs. a "real" reader (in the sense that Chomsky, 1965, projects an ideal native-speaker-hearer). However, we know that there are no ideal readers, that language performance never completely matches the innate competence which Chomsky hypothesizes; readers process written texts idiosyncratically according to their abilities and their knowledge bases. In fact, Fillmore (1982, p. 270) says, "Quite frequently texts are designed to invite idiosyncratic responses in their readers—a situation for which the notion of a corresponding interpretation is thoroughly unwelcome!"

One would be right to question whether a single reader is representative of other readers, except for the fact that we know readers in general are able to make sense of a text, are able to grasp relationships within the text, and are able to agree to a large extent on what a text means.[15] If one reader discerned cohesion in all the written texts analyzed, isn't it reasonable to assume that other readers would as well? On the basis of past experience, that expectation is reasonable. Therefore, it is difficult to dismiss the results of the research reported here. Whatever the degree of variability that exists among a population of readers, it does not undermine the high degree of commonality of interpretation readers are likely to exhibit when tested.

Nevertheless, a reader's sense of cohesion patterns and texture is probably unconscious most of the time. Indirect questions may well call it to their attention. For instance, we might say, "What voice does the narrator take in White's and Didion's essays?" Or, we might ask, "How does Friedman make use of definite articles to create unity?" I suggest that literature teachers who ask students, "Who is *To Kill A Mockingbird* about?" are looking for predominant nodes and the networks that accompany them; that is, they sense that characters create patterns—even though the teachers themselves may not think in terms of patterns. Do "expert" readers such as these literature teachers have a greater sense of pattern and texture than the "average" reader but simply call it by another name?

Composition teachers, also, may be talking about a break in pattern or a flaw in texture when they tell students that their writing doesn't "flow" or is "awkward." It may not flow, for instance, because there are dangling participles due to agent displacement problems or because the node for a particular pronoun is unclear. Can students improve their skills in writing by learning how skilled writers use patterns effectively?

Another pertinent question relates to translating from one language to another. Stine (1980, p.13) says:

---

[15] Where readers do not find a text meaningful, it is a question whether the failure to do so happens because of their insufficient background knowledge or the writer's inability to present ideas with clarity.

> Cohesion within texts differs to such an extent from language to language that translators can work successfully only if they treat the SL [source language] text as a whole unit...while using the cohesive devices of the RL [receptor language] to create an understandable RL text...The goal is that the reader understand the translation in a way as close as possible to the way the reader of the SL understands the text.

Do written texts translated into other languages have similar or different patterns and textures than their English versions?

Do these similarities and differences affect the way persons learn a second language? Undoubtedly so. To learn English, for instance, non-native speakers must learn not only the grammar of the language but cultural assumptions and knowledge as well. Learning definite article placement and interpretation is an example of this difficulty. Because definite articles are very culture-bound, students of the language must constantly add new terminals or establish new frame-nodes in order to interpret them (Stoddard, 1986).

The implications of cohesion and texture in texts have the potential to lead us in several directions, only of few of which have been suggested here. Though some forays may appear to be tangential, what we learn from the venture will contribute to our understanding of the problem space "text."

THE PERSPECTIVE OF TEXTURE

Although text scholars have sensed intuitively that there is texture in texts, little systematic study of its characteristics and its relationship to textual synergism has been done. Bringing this texture to the consciousness of language users is the first task. The perception of cohesion is a reasonable point to begin. There seems to be little doubt that the realization of cohesion and its contribution to the conscious or unconscious perception of texture comes about in readers' minds through a complex process. This means that accounting for just this one text component is not a simple task, and the difficulties multiply manyfold in accounting for texture and textual synergism. One of the first steps, perhaps, is to develop a metalanguage that will more precisely circumscribe the phenomena involved.

This study of texture and its component patterns of cohesion is admittedly tentative and far from holistic. Nevertheless, the results of this research afford preliminary, systematic, and nontrivial insights into cohesion and texture, and hence, the problem space "text." The example of definable cohesion networks provides evidence for the argument that texts do have texture. The graphics developed from cohesion data suggest that the argument is essentially correct.

In the future more sophisticated forms of numerical and graphic heuristics will undoubtedly confirm and expand our present knowledge by testing other components of texture and by testing a more extensive sample of reader-subjects. Such studies should also lead to a greater understanding of the relationship between interpretation of texts and textual synergism. Time will surely temper our understanding of textual truths. If it were not so, further research into the nature of text would be redundant. As it is, describing and explaining the problem space "text" will continue to challenge us.

References

Allerton, D. J. (1978). The notion of givenness and its relation to presupposition and theme. *Lingua, 44,* 133–168.
Anderson, J. R. (1974). Individuation and reference in memory. *Cognitive Psychology, 6,* 495-514.
Anderson, J. R. (1976). *Language, memory, and thought.* Hillsdale, NJ: Lawrence Erlbaum.
Anderson, J. R., & Hastie, R., (1974). Individuation and reference in memory. *Cognitive Psychology, 6,* 495-514.
Ashby, W. R. (1964). *An introduction to cybernetics.* London: John Wiley.
Bach, K., & Harnish, R. M. (1979). *Linguistic communication and speech acts.* Cambridge, MA: MIT Press.
Bailey, R. W. (1981). *Computing in the humanities.* Amsterdam: North-Holland.
Bamberg, B. (1983). What makes a text coherent? *College Composition and Communication, 34,* 417–429.
Barthes, R. (1974). *S/Z.* (Trans. by Richard Miller.) New York: Hill and Wang.
Bellert, I. (1970). On a condition of the coherence of texts. *Semiotica, 2,* (4), 335–363.
Bloomfield, L. (1933). *Language.* New York: Holt, Rinehart and Winston.
Bolinger, D. (1979). Pronouns in discourse. In T. Givon (Ed.), *Discourse and syntax* (pp. 289-309). New York: Academic Press.
Bransford, J. D., & Johnson, M. K. (1973). Consideration of some problems of comprehension. In W. G. Chase (Ed.), *Visual information processing* (pp. 383-438). New York: Academic.
Carrell, P. L. (1982). Cohesion is not coherence. *TESOL Quarterly, 16,* 479-488.
Chafe, W. (1970). *Meaning and the structure of language.* Chicago: University of Chicago Press.
Chafe, W. (1972). Discourse structure and human knowledge. In J. Carroll & R. O. Freedle, (Eds.), *Language comprehension and the acquisition of knowledge* (pp. 41-69). New York: Winston.
Chafe, W. (1976). Givenness, contrastiveness, definiteness, subjects, topics, and point of view. In C. Li (Ed.), *Subject and topic* (pp. 27-55). New York: Academic.
Chafe, W. (1982). Integration and involvement in speaking, writing and oral literature. In D. Tannen (Ed.), *Advances in discourse processes, IX: Spoken and written language: Exploring orality and literacy* (pp 35-53). Norwood, NJ: Ablex.
Charniak, E. (1975, June 10-13). Organization and inference in a frame-like system of common-sense knowledge. In R. C. Schank & B. L. Nash-Webber (Eds.), *Theoretical issues in natural language processing* (pp. 46-58). Cambridge, MA.

Chomsky, N. (1957). *Syntactic structures.* The Hague: Mouton.
Chomsky, N. (1964). Current issues in linguistic theory. In J. A. Fodor & J. J. Katz (Eds.), *The structure of language: Readings in the philosophy of language* (pp. 50-118). Englewood Cliffs, NJ: Prentice-Hall.
Chomsky, N. (1965). *Aspects of the theory of syntax.* Cambridge MA: MIT Press.
Christophersen, P. (1939). *The articles: A study of their theory and use in English.* Copenhagen: Binar Munksgaard.
Clark, H. H. (1973). The language-as-a-fixed effect fallacy: A critique of language statistics in psychological research. *Journal of Verbal Learning and Verbal Behavior, 12,* 335-359.
Clark, H. H. (1977). Bridging. In P. N. Johnson-Laird & P. C. Wason (Eds.), *Thinking: Readings in cognitive science* (pp. 411-420). Cambridge, England: Cambridge University Press.
Clark, H. H. (1978). Inferring what is meant. In W. J. M. Levelt & G. B. Flores d'Arcais (Eds.), *Studies in the perception of language* (pp. 295-322). London: Wiley.
Clark, H. H., & Carlson, T. B. (1981). Context for comprehension. In J. Long & A. Baddeley (Eds.), *Attention and performance IX* (pp. 313-330). Hillsdale, NJ: Lawrence Erlbaum.
Clark, H. H., Carpenter, P. A. & Just, M. A. (1973). On the meeting of semantics and perception. In W. G. Chase (Ed.), *Visual information processing* (pp. 311-381). New York: Academic.
Clark, H. H., & Haviland, S. E. (1974). Psychological processes as linguistic explanation. In D. Cohen (Ed.), *Explaining linguistic phenomena (pp. 91-124).* Washington, DC: Hemisphere.
Clark, H. H., & Haviland, S. E. (1977). Comprehension and the given-new contract. In R. O. Freedle (Ed.), *Advances in discourse processes, I: Discourse production and comprehension* (pp. 1-40). Hillsdale, NJ: Lawrence Erlbaum.
Clark, H. H., & Marshall. C. R. (1981). Definite reference and mutual knowledge. In A. K. Joshi, B. L. Webber, & I. Sag (Eds.), *Elements of discourse understanding* (pp. 10-63). Cambridge: Cambridge University Press.
Clark, H. H., & Sengul, C. J. (1979). In search of referents for nouns and pronouns. *Memory and Cognition, 7,* 35-41.
Collins, A., Brown, J. S. & Larkin, K. M. (1980). Inference in text understanding. In R. J. Spiro, B. C. Bruce, & W. F. Brewer (Eds.), *Theoretical Issues in reading comprehension* (pp. 385-407). Hillsdale, NJ: Lawrence Erlbaum.
Crothers, E . J. (1978). Text inferences. *Discourse Processes, 1,* 51-71.
de Beaugrande, R. (1980). *Advances in discourse processes, IV: Text, discourse, and process.* Norwood, NJ: Ablex.
de Beaugrande, R., & Dressler, W. (1981). *Introduction to textlinguistics.* London: Longman.
Derwing, B. L., Prideaux, G. D., & Baker, W. J. (1980). Introduction: Experimental linguistics in historical perspective. In G. D. Prideaux, B. L. Derwing, & W. J. Baker (Eds.), *Experimental linguistics* (pp. 1-13). Ghent: Story-Scientia.
de Villiers, P. A. (1974). Imagery and theme in recall of connected discourse. *Journal of Experimental Psychology, 103,* 263-268.

Dijk, T. A. van. (1977a). Macro-structures, knowledge frames and discourse comprehension. In P. A. Carpenter & M. A. Just (Eds.), *Cognitive processes in comprehension* (pp. 3-32). Hillsdale, NJ: Lawrence Erlbaum.

Dijk, T. A. van. (1977b). *Text and context: Explorations in the semantics and pragmatics of discourse*. London: Longman.

Dijk, T. A. van., & Kintsch, W. (1977). Cognitive psychology and discourse: Recalling and summarizing stories. In W. Dressler (Ed.), *Current trends in linguistics* (pp. 61-80). Berlin: deGruyter.

Dryer, M. (1976). Generative semantics and the study of discourse structure. *Michigan Linguistic Society Papers, II*, 9-13.

DuBois, J. (1980). Beyond definiteness: The trace of identity in discourse. In W. Chafe, (Ed.), *Advances in discourse processes, II: The pear stories: Cognitive, cultural, and linguistic aspects of narrative production* (pp. 203-274). Norwood, NJ: Ablex.

Eberhart, O. M. Y. (1976). *Elementary students' understanding of certain masculine and neutral generic nouns*. Unpublished doctoral dissertation, Kansas State University, Manhattan, KS.

Ehlich, K. (1982). Anaphora and deixis: Same, similar, or different. In R. J. Jarvella & W. Klein (Eds.), *Speech, place, and action* (pp. 315-338). Chichester: John Wiley and Sons.

Eiler, M. A. (1983). Meaning and choice in writing about literature. In J. Fine & R. O. Freedle (Eds.), *Developmental issues in discourse* (pp. 169-224). Norwood, NJ: Ablex.

Ellegard, A. (1978). The syntactic structure of English: A computer-based study of four kinds of text in the Brown University Corpus. *Gothenburg Studies in English, 43*, 1-116.

Fahnestock, J. (1983). Semantic and lexical coherence. *College composition and communication, 34*, 400-416.

Fillmore, C. (1976). The need for a frame semantics within linguistics. *Statistical Methods in Linguistics*, pp. 5-29.

Fillmore, C. (1981). Pragmatics and the description of discourse. In P. Cole (Ed.), *Radical pragmatics* (pp. 143-166). New York: Academic Press.

Fillmore, C. (1982). Ideal readers and real readers. In D. Tannen (Ed.), *Analyzing discourse: Text and talk* (pp. 248-270). Washington, DC: Georgetown University Press.

Fowler, R. (1981). *Literature as social discourse*. London: Batsford Academic and Educational.

Frederiksen, C. H. (1977). Structure and process in discourse production and comprehension. In P. A. Carpenter & M. A. Just (Eds.), *Cognitive processes in comprehesion* (pp. 313-322). Hillsdale, NJ: Lawrence Erlbaum.

Freeman, D. C. (Ed.). (1970). *Linguistics and literary style*. New York: Holt, Rinehart and Winston.

Freeman, D. C. (1979). Linguistics and error analysis: On agency. In D. McQuade (Ed.), *Linguistics, stylistics, and the teaching of composition* (pp. 143-150). [Special edition of Language and Style.]

Galloway, P. (1978). Testing a theory of narrative structure by computer. In. D. E. Ager, F. E. Knowles, & J. Smith (Eds.), *Advances in computer-aided literary and linguistic research* (pp. 53-58). Birmingham: University of Aston.

Garnham, A. (1987). Understanding Anaphora. In A. W. Ellis (Ed.), *Progress in the psychology of language* (pp. 253-300). London: Lawrence Erlbaum.

Garrod, S. C., & Sanford, A. J. (1977). Interpreting anaphoric relations: The integration of semantic information while reading. *Journal of Verbal Learning and Verbal Behavior, 16,* 77-90.

Garrod, S. C., & Sanford, A. J. (1978). Anaphora: A problem in text comprehension. In R. N. Campbell & P. T. Smith (Eds.), *Recent advances in the psychology of language: Formal and experimental approaches* (pp. 305-314). New York: Plenum.

Garrod, S. C., & Sanford, A. J. (1981). Bridging inferences and the extended domain of reference. In J. Long & A. Baddeley (Eds.), *Attention and performance, IX* (pp. 375-394). Hillsdale, NJ: Lawrence Erlbaum.

Gentner, D. (1981). Verb semantic structures in memory for sentences: Evidence for componential representation. *Cognitive Psychology, 13,* 56-83.

Gibson, W. (1970). Styles and stylistics: A Model T style machine. In D. Freeman (Ed.), *Linguistics and literary style* (pp. 143-164). New York: Holt, Rinehart and Winston.

Goodman, K. S., & Goodman, Y. M. (1977). Learning about psycholinguistic processes by analyzing oral reading. *Harvard Educational Review, 42*(1), 317-333.

Green, G. & Morgan, J. L. (1981). Pragmatics, grammar and discourse. In P. Cole (Ed.), *Radical pragmatics* (pp. 167-182). New York: Academic.

Grice, H. P. (1975). Logic and conversation. In P. Cole & J. Morgan (Eds.), *Syntax and semantics, 3: Speech acts* (pp. 41-58). New York: Academic.

Grimes, J. (1975). *The thread of discourse.* The Hague: Mouton.

Gutwinski, W. (1976). *Cohesion in literary texts: A study of some grammatical and lexical features of English discourse.* The Hague: Mouton.

Haberlandt, K. (1982). Reader expectations in text comprehension. In J. F. Le Ny & W. Kintsch (Eds), *Advances in psychology: Language and comprehension* (pp. 239-249). Amsterdam: North-Holland.

Halliday, M. A. K. (1967). Notes on transitivity and theme in English, part 2. *Journal of Linguistics, 3,* 199-244.

Halliday, M. A. K. (1970). Descriptive linguistics in literary studies. In D. Freeman (Ed.), *Linguistics and literary style* (pp. 57-72). New York: Holt, Rinehart and Winston.

Halliday, M. A. K., & Hasan, R. (1976). *Cohesion in English.* London: Longman.

Hampden-Turner, C. (1981). *Maps of the mind.* New York: Macmillan.

Hankamer, J., & Sag, I. (1976). Deep and surface anaphora. *Linguistic Inquiry, 7*(3), 391-426.

Hasan, R. (1968). *Grammatical cohesion in spoken and written English: Part One. Programme in Linguistics and English Teaching, Paper no. 7.* London: Communication and Research Center.

Hawkins, J. A. (1978). *Definiteness and indefiniteness.* Atlantic Highlands, NJ: Humanities Press.

Hayes, C. W. (1970). A study in prose styles: Edward Gibbon and Ernest Hemingway. In D. Freeman (Ed.), *Linguistics and literary style* (pp. 279-296). New York: Holt, Rinehart and Winston.

Hill, A. A. (1966). A re-examination of the English articles. In F. P. Dineen (Ed.), *17th Annual roundtable* (pp. 217-231). Washington, DC: Georgetown University.

Hirsch, E. D., Jr. (1977). *The philosophy of composition.* Chicago: University of Chicago.

Hrushovski, B. (1982). Integrational semantics. In H. Byrnes (Ed.), *Contemporary perceptions of language* (pp. 156-190). Washington, DC: Georgetown University Press.

Huddleston, R. (1978). On classifying anaphoric relations. A review of Michael A. K. Halliday and Ruqaiya Hasan, Cohesion in English. *Lingua, 45*(3-4), 333-354.

Hunt, M. (1982). *The universe within.* New York: Simon and Schuster.

Jenkinson, T. K., & Weymouth, A. G. (1976). Pronoun usage and explicitness in working-class speech: Toward an evaluative technique. *Language and Speech 19,* (2). 101-116.

Johnson-Laird, P. N. (1983). *Mental models: Towards a cognitive science of language, inference, and consciousness.* Cambridge: Cambridge University Press.

Jones, L. B. (1983). *Pragmatic aspects of English text structure.* Dallas, TX: Summer Institute of Linguistics Publications in Linguistics.

Jordan, M. P. (1983). *Complex lexical cohesion in the English clause and sentence.* Paper presented to the LACUS International Conference, Quebec City, Canada.

Joshi, A. K., & Rosenschein S. J. (1976). Some problems of inferencing: Relation of inferencing to decomposition of predicates. *Statistical Methods in Linguistics,* pp. 47-70.

Kantor, R. N. (1977). *The management and comprehension of discourse connection by pronouns in English.* Unpublished doctoral dissertation. Ohio State University, Columbus OH.

Karttunen, L. (1971). Discourse referents. In J. McCawley (Ed.), *Syntax and semantics, 7: Notes from the linguistic underground* (pp. 363-386). New York: Academic.

Kidd, V. (1971). A study of the images produced through the use of the male pronoun as the generic. *Moments in Contemporary Rhetoric and Communication, 1* (2), 25-30.

Kieras, D. (1977). Problems of reference in text comprehension. In M. Just & P. Carpenter (Eds.), *Cognitive processes in comrehension* (pp. 249-270). Hillsdale, NJ: Lawrence Erlbaum.

Kirsner, R., & Thompson, S. (1976). The role of pragmatic inference in semantics: A study of sensory verb complements in English. *Glossa, 10* (2), 200-237.

Kock, W. K. (1973). Time and text: Toward an adequate heuristics. In J. S. Petofi & H. Rieser (Ed.), *Studies in text grammar* (pp. 113-204). Dordrecht-Holland: D. Reidel.

Kramsky, J. (1972). *The article and the concept of definiteness in language.* The Hague: Mouton.

Kroeber, Karl. (1966). Review of Louis T. Milic's A quantitative approach to the style of Jonathan Swift. *Computers and the Humanities, 1,* 55-58.

Kroeber, Karl. (1967). Computers and research in literary analysis. In E. A. Bowles (Ed.), *Computers in humanistic research* (pp. 135-142). Englewood Cliffs, NJ: Prentice-Hall.

Kroll, B. M., & Van, R. J. (Eds.). (1981). *Exploring speaking and writing relationships: Connections and contrasts.* Urbana, IL: NCTE.

Lakoff, G. (1976). Pronouns and reference. In J. McCawley (Ed.), *Syntax and semantics, 7: Notes from the linguistic underground.* (pp. 275-335). New York: Academic.

Langendoen, D. T. (1966). The syntax of the English expletive "it." In F. P. Dineen (Ed.), *17th Annual roundtable* (pp. 207-216). Washington, DC: Georgetown University.

Leech, G. N., & Short, M. H. (1981). *Style in fiction: A linguistic introduction to English fictional prose.* London: Longman.
Lindemann, B. (1981). Review of text, discourse, and process: Toward a multidisciplinary science of texts. *Journal of Literary Semantics, 10* (2), 120-127.
Longacre, R., & Levinsohn, S. (1977). Field analysis of discourse. In W. U. Dressler (Ed.), *Current trends in textlinguistics* (pp. 103-122). Berlin: deGruyter.
MacKay, D. G. (1983). *Prescriptive grammar and the pronoun problem.* Rowley, MA: Newbury House.
Mackay, D. G., & Fulkerson, D. C. (1979). On the comprehension and production of pronouns. *Journal of Verbal Learning and Verbal Behavior, 18,* 661-673.
Maratsos, M. P. (1976). *The use of definite and indefinite reference in young children.* Cambridge: Cambridge University Press.
Markels, R. Bell. (1983). Cohesion paradigms in paragaphs. *College English, 45*(5). 450-464.
Martyna, W. (1978). What does "he" mean? *Journal of Communication, 28,* 131-38.
Milic, L. T. (1964). *A quantitative approach to the style of Jonathan Swift.* The Hague: Mouton.
Milic, L. T. (1967). Making haste slowly in literary computation. In E. A. Bowles (Ed.), *Computers in humanistic research* (pp.143-152). Englewood Cliffs, NJ: Prentice-Hall.
Milic, L. T. (1970). Connectives in Swift's prose style. In D. Freeman (Ed.), *Linguistics and literary style* (pp. 243-257). New York: Holt, Rinehart and Winston.
Minsky, M. (1975). A framework for representing knowledge. In P. H. Winston (Ed.), *The psychology of computer vision* (pp. 211-277). New York: McGraw-Hill.
Minsky, M. (1982). Music, mind, and meaning. In M. Clynes (Ed.), *Music, mind, and brain* (pp. 1-19). New York: Plenum.
Moskovit, L. (1983). When is broad reference clear? *College Composition and Communication, 34,* 454-469.
Nash, W. (1980). *Designs in prose.* London: Longman.
Norman, D. A. (1982). *Learning and memory.* San Francisco: W. H. Freeman.
Norman, D. A., & Rumelhart, D. E. (1975). *Explorations in cognition.* San Francisco: W. H. Freeman.
Paducheva, E. V. (1970). Anaphoric relations and their representation in the deep structure of a text. In M. Bierwisch & K. E. Heidolph (Eds.), *Progress in linguistics* (pp. 224-232). The Hague: Mouton.
Petofi, J. S. (1969). On the linear patterning of verbal works of art. *Computational Linguistics, 8,* 37-63.
Postal, P. M. (1966). On the so-called "pronouns" in English. In F. P. Dineen (Ed.), *17th Annual Roundtable* (pp. 177-206). Washington, DC: Georgetown University Press.
Reddy, M. (1979). The conduit metaphor—A case of frame conflict in our language about language. In A. Ortony (Ed.), *Metaphor and thought* (pp. 284-324). Cambridge: Cambridge University Press.
Reinhart, T. (1980). Conditions for text coherence. *Poetics Today, 1*(4), 161-180.
Ritchie, G. D. (1980). *Computational grammar: An artificial intelligence approach to linguistic description.* Sussex: Harvester.
Rochester, S. R. (1976). Reference as a speech art: An argument for studying

the listener. In R. N. Campbell, & P. T. Smith (Ed.), *Recent advances in the psychology of language: Formal and experimental approaches* (pp. 335-345). New York: Plenum.

Rochester, S. R., & Martin, J. R. (1977). The art of referring: The speaker's use of noun phrases to instruct the listener. In R. O. Freedle (Ed.), *Advances in discourse processes, I: Discourse production and comprehension* (pp. 245-269). Hillsdale, NJ: Lawrence Erlbaum.

Rumelhart, D. E. (1977). *Introduction to human information processing.* New York: John Wiley and Sons.

Sadock, J. M. (1974). *Toward a linguistic theory of speech acts.* New York: Academic Press.

Sanford, A. J., & Garrod, S. C. (1980). Memory and attention in text comprehension: The problem of reference. In R. Nickerson (Ed.), *Attention and performance VIII* (pp. 459-474). Hillsdale, NJ: Lawrence Erlbaum.

Sanford, A. J., & Garrod, S. C. (1981). *Understanding written language.* Chichester: John Wiley.

Sanford, A. J., & Garrod, S. C. (1982). Toward a processing account of reference. In A. Flammer & W. Kintsch (Eds.), *Advances in psychology, 8: Discourse processing* (pp. 100-110). Amsterdam: North-Holland.

Schank, R. C. (1975, June 10-13). Using knowledge to understand. In R. C. Schank & B. L. Nash-Webber (Eds.), *Theoretical issues in natural language processing.* Cambridge, MA.

Schank, R. C. (1978). Predictive understanding. In R. N. Campbell & P. T. Smith (Eds.), *Recent advances in the psychology of language: Formal and experimental approaches.* (pp. 91-101). New York: Plenum.

Schank, R. C., & Abelson R. P. (1977). *Scripts, plans, goals and understanding: An equiry into knowledge structures.* Hillsdale, NJ: Lawrence Erlbaum.

Schmidt, S. J. (1977). Some problems of communicative text theories. In W. Dressler (Ed.), *Current trends in textlinguistics* (pp. 47-60). Berlin: deGruyter.

Sedelow, S. Y. (1970). Computers in the humanities and fine arts. *Computing Surveys, 2*(2), 89-110.

Sedelow, S. Y., & Sedelow, W. A., Jr. (1966). A preface to computational stylistics. In J. Leed (Ed.), *The computer and literary style* (pp. 1-13). Kent, OH: Kent University.

Simmons, C. (1979). *Cohesion in Russian: The major resource of textual unity.* Unpublished doctoral dissertation, Brown University, Providence, RI.

Stanley [aka Penelope], J. P. (1975). Passive motivation. *Foundations of Language, 13,* 25-39.

Stanley [aka Penelope], J. P. (1978). Target structures and rule conspiracies: Syntactic exploitation. In R. L. Brown, Jr., & M. Steinmann, Jr. (Eds.), *Rhetoric 78* (pp. 387-398). Minneapolis, MN: University of Minnesota Center for Advanced Studies in Language, Style, and Literary Theory.

Stanley [aka Penelope], J. P., & Robbins, S. W. (1977). Forced inference: Uses and abuses of the passive. *Papers in Linguistics, 10* (3-4), 299-311.

Stanley [aka Penelope], J. P., & (Robbins) Wolfe, S. J. (1977). Agent recoverability and truncated passives. *Forum Linguisticum, 2,* 33-46.

Stein, G. (1978). *Studies in the function of the passive.* Tubingen: Gunter Narr.

Stenning, K. (1977). Articles, quantifiers, and their encoding in textual comprehension. In R. O. Freedle (Ed.), *Advances in discourse processing, I: Discourse production and comprehension* (pp. 193-212). Hillsdale, NJ: Lawrence Erlbaum.

Stewart, A H. (1976). *Graphic representation of models in linguistic theory.* Bloomington: Indiana University.

Stine, P. C. (1980). Cohesion in literary texts: A translation problem. *Journal of Literary Semantics, 9,* 13-19.

Stoddard, S. (1981). Beyond counting. In T. Bennett-Kastor (Ed.), *Proceedings of 1981 Mid-America Linguistics Conference* (pp. 267-276). Wichita, KS: Wichita State University.

Stoddard, S. (1983). Is bridging in written texts cohesive? In D. Rood (Ed.), *Proceedings of 1983 Mid-America Linguistics Conference* (pp. 391-399). Boulder, CO: Department of Linguistics, University of Colorado.

Stoddard, S. (1985). Determining the relative cohesiveness of written texts. In E. Johnson (Ed.), *ICEBOL 85: Proceedings of the 1985 International Conference on English Language and Literature Applications of SNOBOL and SPITBOL* (pp. 34-62). Madison, SD: South Dakota State College.

Stoddard, S. (1986). Cultural assumptions, frames, and the allowable economies of English: A cross-cultural problem. In P. Byrd (Ed.), *Teaching across cultures in the university ESL program* (pp. 123-126). Washington, DC: National Association for Foreign Student Affairs.

Stone, V. F. (1979). *The effect of textual cohesion on comprehension of connected discourse.* Unpublished doctoral dissertaton, University of Virginia, Charlottesville, VA.

Stotsky, S. (1983). Types of lexical cohesion in expository writing: Implications for developing the vocabulary of academic discourse. *College Composition and Communication, 34,* 430-446.

Tannen, D. (Ed.). (1982). *Advances in discourse processes, IX: Spoken and written language: Exploring orality and literacy.* Norwood, NJ: Ablex.

Thompson, S. (1983). Grammar and discourse: The English detached participial clause. In F. Klein-Andreu (Ed.), *Discourse perspectives on syntax* (pp. 43-65). New York: Academic.

Thomas, L. (1982, March 14). The art of teaching science. *New York Times Magazine,* pp. 89-93.

Thorndyke, P. W. (1976). The role of inference in discourse comprehension. *Journal of Verbal Learning and Verbal Behavior, 15,* 437-446.

van de Velde, R. G. (1981). Textuality and human reasoning. *Text, 1* (4), 385-406.

Webber, B. L. (1980). Syntax beyond the sentence: Anaphora. In R J. Spiro, B. C. Bruce, & W. F. Brewer (Eds.), *Theoretical issues in reading comprehension: Perspectives from cognitive psychology, linguistics, artificial intelligence, and education* (pp. 141-164). Hillsdale, NJ: Lawrence Erlbaum.

Webber, B. L. (1981). Discourse model synthesis: Preliminaries to reference. In A. K. Joshi, B. L. Webber, & I. Sag (Eds.), *Elements of discourse understanding* (pp. 283-299). Cambridge: Cambridge University Press.

Wender, K. F. (1982). Inference processes in discourse comprehension measured by sentence reading times. In A. Flammer & W. Kintsch (Eds.), *Advances in psychology, 8: Discourse processing* (pp. 166-171). Amsterdam: North-Holland.

Widdowson, H. G. (1975). *Stylistics and the teaching of literature.* London: Longman.

Widdowson, H. G. (1980). Style as meaning. In M. L. Ching, M. C. Haley, & R. F.

Lunsford (Eds.), *Linguistics perspectives on literature* (pp. 235-241). London: Routledge and Kegan Paul.

Winograd, T. (1977). A framework for understanding discourse. In P. A. Carpenter & M. A. Just (Eds.), *Cognitive processes in comprehension* (pp. 63-88). Hillsdale, NJ: Lawrence Erlbaum.

Witte, S. P., & Faigley, L. (1981). Coherence, cohesion, and writing quality. *College composition and Communication, 32,* 189-204.

Appendix A

LIST OF TEXTS ANALYZED

The following, arranged by text-type as they appear in the tables, are the texts used as computer input data. The segments analyzed for definite article, pronoun, and agent displacement cohesion appear on the pages indicated at the end of each entry.

NONFICTION

Baker, Jeffrey J. W., & Allen, Garland E. (1968). *A course in biology* (pp. 16–18 and 288–291). Reading, MA: Addison-Wesley.
Lakoff, Robin. (1975). *Language and woman's place* (pp. 3–6 and 73–76). New York: Harper and Row.
Matthiessen, Peter. (1978). *The snow leopard* (pp. 22–24 and 247–249). New York: Viking.
Sagan, Carl. (1974). *Broca's brain* (pp. 3–5 and 292–294). New York: Random House.
Silverberg, Robert. (1971). *Clocks for the ages: How scientists date the past* (pp. 15–18 and 211–214). New York: MacMillan.
Skinner, Burrus F. (1971). *Beyond freedom and dignity* (pp. 3–6 and 198–202). New York: Alfred A. Knopf.
Stoddard, Robert H. (1982). *Field techniques and research methods in geography* (pp. 1–3 and 115–116). Dubuque, IA: Kendall/Hunt.

ESSAY

Didion, Joan. (1979). In bed. *The white album, 168–172* (pp. 168–172). New York: Simon and Schuster.
Eiseley, Loren. (1971). The brown wasps. *The night country, 227–236* (pp. 227–231). New York: Charles Scribner's Scons.
Friedman, Milton. (1968). Why the American economy is depression-proof. *Dollars and deficits, 72–96* (pp. 86–89). Englewood Cliffs, NJ: Prentice-Hall.
Talese, Gay. (1960). New York. *Esquire, 54,* 37–41 (pp. 37–39).
Thomsen, Dietrick. (1978). The shroud of Turin: A shroud of unknowing. *Science News, 114,* 442–443, 455 (pp. 442–443).
Thurber, James. (1933). University Days. *Vintage, Thurber, vol. II, 197–203* (pp. 197–200). London: Hamish Hamilton.

White, E. B. (1938). Once more to the lake. *One man's meat, 302-311* (pp. 302-306). New York: Harper Bros.

BIOGRAPHY

Angelou, Maya. (1969). *I know why a caged bird sings* (pp. 26-29 and 189-192). New York: Random House.
Gray, Madeline. (1979). *Margaret Sanger: A biography of the champion of birth control* (pp. 77-80 and 381-383). New York: Richard Marek.
Haley, Alex. (Ed.). (1965). *The autobiography of Malcolm X* (pp. 14-16 and 288-290). New York: Grove.
Hodge, Jane Aiken. (1972). *Only a novel: The double life of Jane Austen* (pp. 30-33 and 201-204). Greenwich, CT: Fawcett.
Milford, Nancy. (1970). *Zelda* (pp. 67-72 and 202-205). New York: Harper and Row.
Sandburg, Carl. (1926). *Abraham Lincoln: The prairie years* (pp. 43-46 and 203-206). New York: Harcourt, Brace.
Sandoz, Mari. (1935). *Old Jules* (pp. 2-6 and 392-395). Lincoln, NE: University of Nebraska Press.

NOVEL

Clark, Walter Van Tilburg. (1940). *The ox-bow incident (pp. 3-7 and 105-108). New York: Random House.*
Fitzgerald, F. Scott. (1925). *The great Gatsby (pp. 1-4 and 164-168). New York: Charles Scribner's Sons.*
Hemingway, Ernest. (1940). *For whom the bell tolls* (pp. 59-63 and 228-231). New York: Charles Scribner's Sons.
Kesey, Ken. (1962). *One flew over the cuckoo's nest* (pp. 25-27 and 249-251). New York: Viking.
Lee, Harper. (1960). *To kill a mockingbird* (pp. 11-14 and 281-284). Philadelphia: J. B. Lippincott.
London, Jack. (1904). *The sea-wolf* (pp. 17-20 and 217-220). New York: MacMillan.
Safire, William. (1977). *Full disclosure* (pp. 115-118 and 328-330). Garden City, NJ: Doubleday.

SHORT STORY

Bradbury, Ray. (1958). August 2002: Night meeting. *The Martian chronicles, 102-110* (pp. 102-106). Garden City, NJ: Doubleday.
Faulkner, William. (1930). Dry September. *Collected stories of William Faulkner, 169-184* (pp. 169-174). New York: Random House.

Hammett, Dashiell. (1932). They can only hang you once. *The adventures of Sam Spade and other stories, 36–55* (pp. 36–39). Cleveland: World.

O'Connor, Flannery. (1953). A good man is hard to find. *A good man is hard to find, 11–29* (pp. 11–15). Garden City, NJ: Doubleday.

Porter, Katherine Anne. (1930). The jilting of Granny Weatherall. *Flowering Judas and other stories, 121–136* (pp. 121–126). New York: Harcourt, Brace.

Rivers, Diana. (1981). Family reunion. *Lesbian Fiction* (Ed. by Elly Bulkin, 63–76) (pp. 63–66). Watertown, MA: Persephone.

Steinbeck, John. (1933). The chrysanthemums. *The long valley, 1–12* (pp. 1–4). New York: Bantam.

Appendix B

ABBREVIATIONS OF COLUMN HEADINGS FOR TABLES

AgD = Agent Displacement Cohesion
CE = Cohesive Element
CEI = -ing Cohesive Element
CEP = Passive Cohesive Element
CI = Cohesion Index
Def = Definite Article Cohesion
Dist = Distance in Words
FCE = Fulfilled Cohesive Element
Pro = Pronoun Cohesion
SCI = Summary Cohesion Index
UCE = Unfulfilled Cohesive Element
UCEI = Unfulfilled -ing Cohesive Element
UCEP = Unfulfilled Passive Cohesive Element

Table A. Occurrences of Definite Articles–Nonfiction.

	Words	Nodes	CE	UCE	%NODES/ WORDS	%CE/ WORDS	%UCE/ CE
Baker/Allen 1	859	44	75	7	5.12	8.73	9.33
Baker Allen 2	951	50	86	15	5.26	9.04	17.44
Lakoff 1	1001	37	59	12	3.70	5.89	20.34
Lakoff 2	1005	33	49	6	3.28	4.88	12.24
Matthiessen 1	942	33	73	18	3.50	7.75	24.66
Matthiessen 2	1019	28	74	39	2.75	7.26	52.70
Sagan 1	924	33	56	4	3.57	6.06	7.14
Sagan 2	883	39	75	9	4.42	8.49	12.00
Silverberg 1	925	41	94	10	4.43	10.16	10.64
Silverberg 2	857	29	50	10	3.38	5.83	20.00
Skinner 1	922	25	42	10	2.71	4.56	23.81
Skinner 2	1020	35	65	13	3.43	6.37	20.00
Stoddard 1	900	37	78	15	4.11	8.67	19.23
Stoddard 2	941	44	71	0	4.68	7.55	0.00
All texts, fulfilled CE only						5.92	
All texts, all CE					3.86	7.20	17.74
Median percentage, all CE					3.93	7.50	13.89

Source: By Author

Table B. Occurrences of Definite Articles–Essay.

	Words	Nodes	CE	UCE	%NODES/ WORDS	%CE/ WORDS	%UCE/ CE
Didion	1369	39	69	19	2.85	5.04	27.54
Eiseley	1435	42	106	14	2.93	7.39	13.21
Friedman	1232	59	120	12	4.79	9.74	10.00
Talese	1087	28	58	12	2.58	5.34	20.69
Thomsen	1302	45	115	20	3.46	8.83	17.39
Thurber	1471	36	60	3	2.44	4.08	5.00
White	1533	50	172	28	3.26	11.22	16.28
All texts, fulfilled CE only						6.28	
All texts, all CE					3.17	7.38	15.43
Median percentage, all CE					2.93	7.39	16.28

Source: By Author

Table C. Occurrences of Definite Articles–Biography

	Words	Nodes	CE	UCE	%NODES/ WORDS	%CE/ WORDS	%UCE/ CE
Angelou 1	889	26	69	9	2.92	7.76	13.04
Angelou 2	871	21	37	8	2.41	4.25	21.62
Gray 1	946	21	33	9	2.22	3.49	27.27
Gray 2	734	23	43	14	3.13	5.86	32.56
Haley 1	1014	19	36	12	1.87	3.55	33.33
Haley 2	864	17	47	24	1.97	5.44	51.06
Hodge 1	863	34	68	18	3.94	7.88	26.47
Hodge 2	906	27	45	13	2.98	4.97	28.89
Milford 1	1008	26	52	7	2.58	5.16	13.46
Milford 2	910	28	59	4	3.08	6.48	6.78
Sandburg 1	1141	61	98	22	5.35	8.59	22.45
Sandburg 2	724	29	64	25	4.01	8.84	39.06
Sandoz 1	936	31	91	28	3.31	9.72	30.77
Sandoz 2	937	34	93	21	3.63	9.93	22.58
All texts, fulfilled CE only						4.87	
All texts, all CE					3.12	6.55	25.63
Median percentage, all CE					2.82	6.02	27.43

Source: By Author

Text and Texture: Patterns of Cohesion

Table D. Occurrences of Definite Articles–Novel

	Words	Nodes	CE	UCE	%NODES/WORDS	%CE/WORDS	%UCE/CE
Clark 1	1021	21	100	54	2.06	9.79	54.00
Clark 2	1174	15	40	22	1.28	3.41	55.00
Fitzgerald 1	1014	25	55	21	2.47	5.42	38.18
Fitzgerald 2	963	22	40	7	2.28	4.15	17.50
Hemingway 1	1133	27	116	55	2.38	10.24	47.41
Hemingway 2	1005	20	50	19	1.99	4.98	38.00
Kesey 1	1047	34	59	11	3.25	5.64	18.64
Kesey 2	1078	24	71	6	2.23	6.59	22.54
Lee 1	950	16	35	3	1.68	3.68	8.57
Lee 2	954	11	19	5	1.15	1.99	26.32
London 1	1069	30	88	12	2.81	8.23	13.64
London 2	918	23	63	11	2.51	6.86	17.46
Safire 1	927	21	84	32	2.66	9.06	38.10
Safire 2	981	34	76	21	3.47	7.75	27.63
All texts, fulfilled CE only						4.37	
All texts, all CE					2.29	6.34	31.14
Median percentage, all CE					2.38	6.42	29.47

Source: By Author

Table E. Occurrences of Definite Articles–Short Story.

	Words	Nodes	CE	UCE	%NODES/WORDS	%CE/WORDS	%UCE/CE
Bradbury	1494	27	87	16	1.81	5.82	18.39
Faulkner	1467	30	99	22	2.04	6.75	22.22
Hammett	1359	26	78	12	1.91	5.74	15.38
O'Connor	1558	31	101	42	1.99	6.48	41.58
Porter	1428	17	46	22	1.19	3.22	47.83
Rivers	1462	26	60	14	1.78	4.10	23.33
Steinbeck	1353	36	97	8	2.66	7.17	8.25
All texts, fulfilled CE only						4.27	
All texts, all CE					1.91	5.61	23.94
Median percentage, all CE					1.91	5.82	22.22

Source: By Author

Table F. Occurrences of Pronouns–Nonfiction.

	Words	Nodes	CE	UCE	%NODES/ WORDS	%CE/ WORDS	%UCE/ CE
Baker/Allen 1	893	6	6	0	.67	.67	0.00
Baker Allen 2	962	16	21	1	1.66	2.18	4.76
Lakoff 1	1001	20	65	25	2.00	6.49	38.46
Lakoff 2	1015	20	35	13	1.97	3.44	27.14
Matthiessen 1	955	19	56	15	1.99	5.86	26.79
Matthiessen 2	1027	19	75	11	1.85	7.30	14.67
Sagan 1	936	13	31	9	1.39	3.31	29.03
Sagan 2	897	14	31	13	1.56	3.46	41.94
Silverberg 1	947	15	33	12	1.58	3.48	36.36
Silverberg 2	866	14	20	2	1.62	2.31	10.00
Skinner 1	919	18	58	32	1.96	6.31	55.17
Skinner 2	1025	24	72	16	2.34	7.02	22.22
Stoddard 1	905	14	21	2	1.55	2.32	9.52
Stoddard 2	946	13	22	0	1.37	2.33	0.00
All texts, fulfilled CE only						2.97	
All texts, all CE					1.69	4.11	27.66
Median percentage, all CE					1.60	3.38	26.42

Source: By Author

Table G. Occurrences of Pronouns–Essay.

	Words	Nodes	CE	UCE	%NODES/ WORDS	%CE/ WORDS	%UCE/ CE
Didion	1374	19	108	1	1.38	7.86	.93
Eiseley	1441	26	95	9	1.80	6.59	9.47
Friedman	1283	17	34	4	1.33	2.65	11.77
Talese	1114	20	46	5	1.80	4.13	10.87
Thomsen	1339	29	44	3	2.17	3.29	6.82
Thurber	1481	33	188	31	2.23	12.69	16.49
White	1540	27	107	10	1.75	6.95	9.35
All texts, fulfilled only						5.84	
All texts, all CE					1.79	6.50	10.13
Median percentage, all CE					1.80	6.59	9.47

Source: By Author

Table H. Occurrences of Pronouns–Biography

	Words	Nodes	CE	UCE	%NODES/WORDS	%CE/WORDS	%UCE/CE
Angelou 1	879	25	86	3	2.84	9.78	3.49
Angelou 2	875	28	87	1	3.20	9.94	1.15
Gray 1	955	21	104	0	2.20	10.89	0.00
Gray 2	791	16	26	0	2.02	3.29	0.00
Haley 1	1016	27	135	8	2.66	13.29	5.93
Haley 2	882	22	79	0	2.49	8.96	0.00
Hodge 1	977	21	41	4	2.15	4.20	9.76
Hodge 2	909	24	54	9	2.64	5.94	16.67
Milford 1	1012	43	73	1	4.25	7.21	1.37
Milford 2	896	31	83	4	3.46	9.26	4.82
Sandburg 1	1145	26	100	2	2.27	8.73	2.00
Sandburg 2	766	16	36	0	2.09	4.70	0.00
Sandoz 1	968	17	50	4	1.76	5.17	8.00
Sandoz 2	946	25	73	3	2.64	7.72	4.11
All texts, fulfilled only						7.59	
All texts, all CE					2.63	7.89	3.80
Median percentage, all CE					2.39	7.45	3.21

Source: By Author

Table I. Occurrences of Pronouns–Novel

	Words	Nodes	CE	UCE	%NODES/WORDS	%CE/WORDS	%UCE/CE
Clark 1	1030	19	60	1	1.84	5.83	1.67
Clark 2	1170	22	155	11	1.88	13.24	7.10
Fitzgerald 1	1028	20	98	5	1.95	9.53	5.10
Fitzgerald 2	960	23	114	18	2.40	11.88	15.79
Hemingway 1	1136	23	104	14	2.02	9.15	13.46
Hemingway 2	1013	24	131	13	2.37	12.93	9.92
Kesey 1	1050	20	114	5	1.90	10.86	4.39
Kesey 2	1083	29	95	6	2.68	8.77	6.32
Lee 1	951	36	133	4	3.79	13.98	3.01
Lee 2	934	46	193	29	4.93	20.66	15.03
London 1	1074	22	83	5	2.05	7.73	6.02
London 2	913	33	92	13	3.61	10.08	14.13
Safire 1	954	22	82	5	2.31	8.60	6.10
Safire 2	1009	27	56	4	2.68	5.55	7.14
All texts, fulfilled CE only						9.60	
All texts, all CE					2.47	10.48	8.81
Median percentage, all CE					2.26	9.80	10.12

Source: By Author

Table J. Occurrences of Pronoun-Short Story.

	Words	Nodes	CE	UCE	%NODES/ WORDS	%CE/ WORDS	%UCE/ CE
Bradbury	1508	40	146	17	2.65	9.68	11.64
Faulkner	1479	49	173	25	3.31	11.70	14.45
Hammett	1325	54	146	10	4.08	11.02	6.85
O'Connor	1455	50	156	13	3.44	10.72	8.83
Porter	1418	37	175	4	2.61	12.34	2.29
Rivers	1463	38	171	12	2.60	11.69	7.02
Steinbeck	1359	35	129	9	2.58	9.49	6.98
All texts, fulfilled CE only						10.05	
All texts, all CE					3.03	10.95	8.21
Median percentage, all CE					2.65	11.02	7.02

Source: By Author

Table K. Occurrences of Agent Displacements-Nonfiction.

	Words	Nodes	CEP	CEI	UCEP	UCEI	%NODES/ WORDS	%CE/ WORDS	%UCEP/ CE	%UCEI/ CE
Baker/Allen 1	879	15	17	19	13	4	1.71	4.09	76.47	21.05
Baker Allen 2	943	20	17	18	10	2	2.12	3.71	58.82	11.11
Lakoff 1	982	17	20	18	13	1	1.73	3.87	65.00	5.56
Lakoff 2	1007	14	16	14	11	1	1.39	2.98	68.75	7.14
Matthiessen 1	956	19	11	21	6	2	1.99	3.35	54.55	9.52
Matthiessen 2	1025	13	10	17	5	1	1.27	3.64	50.00	5.88
Sagan 1	920	19	34	31	29	6	2.06	7.07	85.29	19.35
Sagan 2	913	7	13	6	12	0	.77	2.08	92.31	0.00
Silverberg 1	942	12	5	17	5	3	1.27	2.33	100.00	17.65
Silverberg 2	846	10	29	21	23	12	1.18	5.91	79.31	57.14
Skinner 1	904	16	12	15	4	1	1.77	2.99	33.33	6.67
Skinner 2	1000	15	28	12	23	2	1.50	4.00	82.14	16.67
Stoddard 1	892	15	21	23	19	10	1.68	4.93	90.48	43.48
Stoddard 2	929	15	20	41	10	5	1.61	6.56	50.00	12.20
All texts, fulfilled CE only							2.21			
All texts, all CE							1.58	4.00	72.33	19.05
Median percentage, all CE							1.62	3.90	67.65	16.22

Source: By Author

Table L. Occurrences of Agent Displacements–Essay.

	Words	Nodes	CEP	CEI	UCEP	UCEI	%NODES/ WORDS	%CE/ WORDS	%UCEP/ CE	%UCEI/ CE
Baker/Allen 1	879	15	17	19	13	4	1.71	4.09	76.47	21.05
Didion	1368	19	15	23	11	2	1.39	2.78	73.33	8.70
Eiseley	1436	28	16	36	12	5	1.95	3.62	75.00	13.89
Friedman	1261	13	14	20	11	2	1.03	2.70	78.57	10.00
Talese	1112	24	19	24	13	1	2.16	3.87	68.42	4.17
Thomsen	1303	17	38	18	30	7	1.30	4.30	78.95	38.89
Thurber	1478	27	17	30	11	4	1.83	3.18	64.71	13.33
White	1528	21	16	29	14	3	1.37	2.95	87.50	10.34
Allo texts, fulfilled CE only								1.99		
All texts, all CE							1.57	3.32	75.56	13.33
Median percentage, all CE							1.39	3.18	75.00	10.34

Source: By Author

Table M. Occurrences of Agent Displacements–Biography.

	Words	Nodes	CEP	CEI	UCEP	UCEI	%NODES/ WORDS	%CE/ WORDS	%UCEP/ CE	%UCEI/ CE
Angelou 1	920	15	5	17	0	1	1.63	2.39	0.00	5.88
Angelou 2	872	13	14	15	12	1	1.49	3.33	85.71	6.67
Gray 1	945	12	15	26	10	0	1.27	4.34	66.67	0.00
Gray 2	764	17	23	18	15	2	2.23	5.37	65.22	11.11
Haley 1	1011	24	6	32	6	2	2.37	3.76	100.00	6.25
Haley 2	876	16	13	14	9	1	1.83	2.96	69.23	7.69
Hodge 1	989	10	8	14	7	4	1.01	2.23	87.50	28.57
Hodge 2	908	9	7	12	6	0	.99	2.09	85.71	0.00
Milford 1	1011	22	11	22	7	0	2.18	3.27	63.64	0.00
Milford 2	910	19	14	13	5	0	2.09	2.97	35.71	0.00
Sandburg 1	1155	18	3	48	2	0	1.56	4.42	66.67	0.00
Sandburg 2	755	16	11	25	9	2	2.12	4.77	81.82	8.00
Sandoz 1	960	19	14	15	6	1	1.98	3.02	42.86	6.67
Sandoz 2	945	16	6	22	5	3	1.69	2.96	83.33	13.64
All texts, fulfilled CE only								2.51		
All texts, all CE							1.74	3.40	66.00	6.01
Median percentage, all CE							1.78	3.12	65.79	6.25

Source: By Author

Table N. Occurrences of Agent Displacements–Novel.

	Words	Nodes	CEP	CEI	UCEP	UCEI	%NODES/ WORDS	%CE/ WORDS	%UCEP/ CE	%UCEI/ CE
Clark 1	1018	18	21	19	16	1	1.87	3.99	76.19	5.56
Clark 2	1167	10	9	29	6	6	.86	3.26	66.67	20.69
Fitzgerald 1	1021	13	13	12	9	3	1.27	2.45	69.23	25.00
Fitzgerald 2	949	9	13	5	9	0	.95	1.90	69.23	0.00
Hemingway 1	1138	11	12	14	11	1	.97	2.28	91.67	7.14
Hemingway 2	1008	5	11	9	9	5	.50	1.98	81.82	55.56
Kesey 1	1044	11	13	15	6	0	1.05	2.67	46.15	0.00
Kesey 2	1076	21	11	50	9	5	1.95	5.67	81.82	10.00
Lee 1	958	6	5	9	5	1	.63	1.46	100.00	11.11
Lee 2	948	6	3	5	1	0	.63	.85	33.33	0.00
London 1	1062	21	13	20	7	0	1.98	3.10	53.85	0.00
London 2	917	15	8	12	0	0	1.64	2.18	0.00	0.00
Safire 1	938	14	15	18	12	1	1.49	3.52	80.00	5.56
Safire 2	1000	15	10	15	4	2	1.50	2.50	40.00	13.33
All texts, fulfilled CE only								1.83		
All texts, all CE							1.23	2.73	66.24	10.78
Median percentage, all CE							1.28	2.68	69.23	9.09

Source: By Author

Table O. Occurrences of Agent Displacements–Short Story.

	Words	Nodes	CEP	CEI	UCEP	UCEI	%NODES/ WORDS	%CE/ WORDS	%UCEP/ CE	%UCEI/ CE
Bradbury	1505	25	10	31	6	0	1.66	2.72	60.00	0.00
Faulkner	1478	26	16	21	9	1	1.76	2.50	56.25	4.76
Hammett	1344	18	12	22	9	1	1.34	2.53	75.00	4.55
O'Connor	1568	15	4	18	2	2	.96	1.41	50.00	11.11
Porter	1417	15	14	25	7	0	1.06	2.75	50.00	0.00
Rivers	1453	29	18	34	9	0	2.00	3.58	50.00	0.00
Steinbeck	1355	22	19	22	8	1	1.62	3.02	42.11	4.55
All texts, fulfilled CE only								2.08		
All texts, all CE							1.48	2.63	53.76	2.89
Median percentage, all CE							1.62	2.72	50.00	4.55

Source: By Author

128 Text and Texture: Patterns of Cohesion

Table P. Cohesion Index Factors–Nonfiction

	Def Dist/FCE	Def FCE/Nodes	Pro Dist/FCE	Pro FCE/Nodes	AgD Dist/FCE	AgD FCE/Nodes
Baker 1	46.51	1.55	12.33	1.00	33.05	1.27
Baker 2	20.25	1.42	9.90	1.25	16.70	1.15
Lakoff 1	26.60	1.27	54.78	2.20	13.21	1.41
Lakoff 2	37.77	1.30	5.41	1.10	12.11	1.29
Matthiessen 1	50.80	1.67	167.44	2.16	10.75	1.00
Matthiessen 2	28.34	1.25	264.92	3.37	11.33	1.62
Sagan 1	82.96	1.58	38.27	1.69	29.17	1.58
Sagan 2	48.53	1.69	9.00	1.29	23.00	1.00
Silverberg 1	28.82	2.05	18.43	1.40	13.33	1.17
Silverberg 2	25.53	1.38	9.28	1.29	22.20	1.50
Skinner 1	26.56	1.28	9.77	1.44	14.95	1.38
Skinner 2	15.67	1.49	16.30	2.33	4.67	1.00
Stoddard 1	42.95	1.70	8.26	1.36	4.80	1.00
Stoddard 2	85.13	1.61	35.68	1.69	69.07	3.07
All Texts	41.89	1.53	76.12	1.76	24.91	1.41

Source: By Author

Table Q. Cohesion Index Factors–Essay.

	Def Dist/FCE	Def FCE/Nodes	Pro Dist/FCE	Pro FCE/Nodes	AgD Dist/FCE	AgD FCE/Nodes
Didion	25.04	1.28	454.57	5.63	63.08	1.23
Eiseley	117.48	2.19	561.98	3.31	7.97	1.25
Friedman	144.14	1.83	126.27	1.76	15.28	1.62
Talese	27.93	1.64	24.54	2.05	5.53	1.21
Thomsen	79.87	2.11	13.12	1.41	13.26	1.12
Thurber	98.05	1.58	322.87	4.76	22.07	1.19
White	94.85	2.88	319.40	3.59	7.46	1.33
All Texts	94.17	1.98	329.11	3.27	18.35	1.27

Source: By Author

Table R. Cohesion Index Factors–Biography.

	Def Dist/FCE	Def FCE/Nodes	Pro Dist/FCE	Pro FCE/Nodes	AgD Dist/FCE	AgD FCE/Nodes
Angelou 1	53.27	2.31	103.27	3.32	23.48	1.40
Angelou 2	22.10	1.38	157.85	3.07	11.44	1.23
Gray 1	21.83	1.14	121.04	4.95	144.00	2.58
Gray 2	45.72	1.26	15.77	1.63	13.42	1.41
Haley 1	33.58	1.26	308.01	4.70	13.53	1.25
Haley 2	14.74	1.35	290.63	3.59	16.82	1.06
Hodge 1	25.62	1.47	26.62	1.76	13.73	1.10
Hodge 2	38.81	1.19	22.31	1.88	9.38	1.44
Milford 1	100.20	1.73	25.25	1.67	4.38	1.18
Milford 2	104.71	1.96	17.29	2.55	35.50	1.16
Sandburg 1	28.71	1.25	154.72	3.77	57.73	2.72
Sandburg 2	11.74	1.34	41.06	2.25	29.24	1.56
Sandoz 1	22.41	2.03	22.91	2.71	9.91	1.16
Sandoz 2	46.21	2.12	30.44	2.80	12.95	1.25
All Texts	45.50	1.56	123.93	2.89	34.74	1.45

Source: By Author

Table S. Cohesion Index Factors–Novel.

	Def Dist/FCE	Def FCE/Nodes	Pro Dist/FCE	Pro FCE/Nodes	AgD Dist/FCE	AgD FCE/Nodes
Clark 1	47.28	2.19	115.39	3.11	85.91	1.28
Clark 2	15.00	1.20	269.35	6.55	304.38	2.89
Fitzgerald 1	19.88	1.36	336.98	4.65	4.69	1.15
Fitzgerald 2	50.21	1.50	183.95	4.17	12.56	1.10
Hemingway 1	161.67	2.26	83.86	3.91	35.09	1.27
Hemingway 2	41.19	1.55	223.25	4.92	7.17	1.20
Kesey 1	74.23	1.41	126.02	5.45	58.91	2.00
Kesey 1	138.94	2.71	46.30	3.07	68.89	2.23
Lee 1	47.63	2.00	85.78	3.58	4.13	1.33
Lee 2	17.07	1.27	78.00	3.57	130.86	1.67
London 1	110.71	2.53	149.05	3.55	11.54	1.24
London 2	129.37	2.26	125.71	2.39	25.15	1.33
Safire 1	203.13	2.48	46.04	3.50	26.05	1.43
Safire 2	32.76	1.62	28.34	1.93	13.68	1.27
All Texts	96.50	1.91	143.71	3.87	68.33	1.49

Source: By Author

Table T. Cohesion Index Factors–Short Story.

	Def Dist/FCE	Def FCE/Nodes	Pro Dist/FCE	Pro FCE/Nodes	AgD Dist/FCE	AgD FCE/Nodes
Bradbury	102.70	2.63	46.40	3.23	21.63	1.40
Faulkner	305.03	2.57	143.82	3.02	10.85	1.04
Hammett	111.70	2.54	31.40	2.52	11.08	1.33
O'Connor	77.03	1.90	40.11	2.86	7.56	1.20
Porter	37.46	1.41	93.01	4.62	116.25	2.13
Rivers	249.41	1.77	448.09	4.18	43.00	1.48
Steinbeck	135.17	2.47	54.03	3.43	35.13	1.36
All Texts	155.32	2.24	130.13	3.32	38.60	1.41

Source: By Author

Appendix C

EXCEPT FROM SNOBOL4 COMPUTER PROGRAM

```
*       THE FIRST PART OF THE PROGRAM IDENTIFIES CATEGORIES:   WORD, SPECIFIC
*       NODE, INDEFINITE ARTICLE, DEFINITE ARTICLE, DEMONSTRATIVE, AND
*       GENERAL WORD.  IT FURTHER ASSIGNS THESE TO TABLES.
21
22  NEXT.CARD   CARD = ' ' INPUT ' '                           :F(FIND.DIST)
23              OUTPUT = TEMP
24              OUTPUT =
25              OUTPUT = CARD
26              TEMP = CARD
27  AGAIN       CARD BREAK(PUNC) . WORD  SPAN(PUNC) =          :F(NEXT.CARD)
28     +        IDENT(WORD)                                    :S(AGAIN)
29              NUM.WORD = NUM.WORD + 1
30
31  FIND.SPN    WORD SPAN('*') BREAK('*') . SPN                :F(FIND.INDEF)
32              NUM.SPN = NUM.SPN + 1
33              SPN.T<SPN> = SPN.T<SPN> + 1
34              SPN.LOC.T<NUM.WORD> = SPN
35
36  FIND.INDEF  WORD SPAN('@') BREAK('@') . INDEF              :F(FIND.DEF)
37              NUM.INDEF = NUM.INDEF + 1
38              INDEF.T<INDEF> = INDEF.T<INDEF> + 1
39              INDEF.LOC.T<INDEF> = NUM.WORD                  :(AGAIN)
40
41  FIND.DEF    WORD SPAN('/') BREAK('/') . DEF                :F(FIND.DEM)
42              NUM.DEF = NUM.DEF + 1
43              DEF.T<DEF> = DEF.T<DEF> + 1
44              DEF DIGITS . DEF.NO
45              DEF.LOC.T<NUM.WORD> = GT(DEF.NO,0) DEF         :S(AGAIN)
46
47              EX = EQ(DEF.NO,0) DEF
48              EX.LOC.T<NUM.WORD> = EX
49              NUM.EX = NUM.EX + 1                            :(AGAIN)
50  FIND.DEM    WORD SPAN('&') BREAK('&') . DEM                :F(FIND.GWD)
51              NUM.DEM = NUM.DEM + 1
52              DEM.T<DEM> = DEM.T<DEM> + 1                    :(AGAIN)
53  FIND.GWD    WORD POS(0) CHAR . GWD
54              GWD = ' ' GWD
55              TEMP GWD = DUPL(' ',SIZE(GWD))                 :(AGAIN)
56
*       THE SECOND PART OF THE PROGRAM CONVERTS TABLES TO ARRAYS AND CALCULATE S
*       DISTANCES BETWEEN SPECIFIC NODES AND DEFINITE ARTICLES REFERRING
*       TO THEM.
57
58  FIND.DIST   SPN.LOC.ARR = CONVERT(SPN.LOC.T,'ARRAY')
59              DEF.LOC.ARR = CONVERT(DEF.LOC.T,'ARRAY')
60  ADD1        S.LINE = S.LINE + 1
61              SPN.LOC.ARR<S.LINE,2> DIGITS . SPN.NO          :F(STAT)
62              D.LINE = 0
63  ADD2        D.LINE = D.LINE + 1
64              DEF.LOC.ARR<D.LINE,2> DIGITS . SPDEF.NO        :F(ADD1)
65              SPDEF.DIST = IDENT(SPN.NO,SPDEF.NO) DEF.LOC.ARR<D.LINE,1> -
       +                    SPN.LOC.ARR<S.LINE,1> - 1          :F(ADD2)
66              SPDEF.DIST = LT(SPDEF.DIST,0) SPDEF.DIST + 2
67
68              OUTPUT = 'DISTANCE FOR ' DEF.LOC.ARR<D.LINE,2> ' AT '
       +                 DEF.LOC.ARR<D.LINE,1> ' IS ' SPDEF.DIST ' WORDS.'
69              SPDIST = SPDIST + 1                            :(ADD2)
70
*       THE THIRD PART OF THE PROGRAM CALCULATES CERTAIN STATISTICS RELEVANT
*       TO THE STUDY AND SPECIFIES THE OUTPUT.
```

Author Index

A
Abelson, R.P., 23, 49, *114*
Allerton, D.J., *108*
Anderson, J.R., 49, *108*
Ashby, W.R., 1, 48, *108*

B
Bach, K., 16, *108*
Bailey, R.W., *108*
Baker, W.J., *109*
Bamberg, B., 10, *108*
Barthes, R., 89, 101, *108*
Bellert, I., *108*
Bloomfield, L., *108*
Bolinger, D., 22, *108*
Bransford, J.D., *108*
Brown, J.S., 101, *109*

C
Carlson, T.B., 10, *109*
Carpenter, P.A., *109*
Carrell, P.L., 14, *108*
Chafe, W., 33, 36, 37, *108*
Charniak, E., *108*
Chomsky, N., 60, 105, *109*
Christophersen, P., 54, *109*
Clark, H.H., 3, 10, 21, 23, 25, 28, 33, 36, 40, 54, *109*
Collins, A., 101, *109*
Crothers, E.J., *109*

D
de Beaugrande, R., 3, 10, 14, 19, 33, 35, 36, 41, 42, *109*
Derwing, B.L., *109*
de Villiers, P.A., *109*
Dressler, W., 10, 14, 19, *109*
Dryer, M., *110*
DuBois, J., 33, 36, 38, *110*

E
Eberhart, O.M.Y., 41, *110*
Ehlich, K., *110*
Eiler, M.A., 13, *110*
Ellegard, A., 46, 49, *110*

F
Fahnestock, J., 10, *110*
Faigley, L., 10, 21, *116*
Fillmore, C., 45, 93, 105, *110*
Fowler, R., 7, 9, *110*
Frederiksen, C.H., 13, 14, *110*
Freeman, D.C., 43, *110*
Fulkerson, D.L., 41, *113*

G
Galloway, P., 49, *110*
Garnham, A., 20, *110*
Garrod, S.C., 24, 26, 35, *111, 114*
Gentner, D., 26, 35, 40, 98, 101, *111*
Gibson, W., 55, *111*
Goodman, K., 16, 22, *111*
Goodman, Y., 16, 22, *111*
Green, G., 2, 10, 11, 20, 22, 27, *111*
Grice, H.P., 16, 35, *111*
Grimes, J., 22, 54, 101, *111*
Gutwinski, W., 28, 38, 46, 101, *111*

H
Haberlandt, K., *111*
Halliday, M.A.K., 3, 6, 7, 10, 11, 14, 16, 17, 18, 21, 22, 23, 28, 30, 32, 33, 41, 54, 55, 101, *111*
Hampden-Turner, C., 7, *111*
Hankamer, J., 3, 21, *111*
Harnish, R.M., 16, *108*
Hasan, R., 3, 6, 7, 10, 11, 14, 16, 17, 18, 21, 22, 23, 28, 30, 32, 33, 41, 54, 101, *111*
Hastie, R., *108*

Haviland, S.E., 10, *109*
Hawkins, J.A., 33, 37, 54, *111*
Hayes, C.W., 55, *111*
Hill, A.A., *111*
Hirsch, E.D., *111*
Hrushovski, B., 2, 3, 20, 25, 35, 46, *112*
Huddleston, R., *112*
Hunt, M., *112*

J
Jenkinson, T.K., *112*
Johnson, M.K., *108*
Johnson-Laird, P.N., *112*
Jones, L.B., *112*
Jordan, M.P., 22, *112*
Joshi, A.K., *112*
Just, M.A., *109*

K
Kantor, R.N., 9, *112*
Karttunen, L., *112*
Kidd, V., 41, *112*
Kieras, D., *112*
Kintsch, W., *110*
Kirsner, R., 28, *112*
Kock, W.K., 46, *112*
Kramsky, J., *112*
Kroeber, K., 45, 49, *112*
Kroll, B.M., *112*

L
Lakoff, G., 25, 26, 40, 69, 99, *112*
Langendoen, D.T., *112*
Larkin, K.M., 101, *109*
Leech, G.N., 18, *113*
Levinsohn, S., *113*
Lindemann, B., *113*
Longacre, R., *113*

M
Mackay, D.G., 41, *113*
Maratsos, M.P., *113*
Markels, R.B., 7, 10, 14, 19, *113*
Marshall, C.R., 33, *109*
Martin, J.R., 33, 36, *114*
Martyna, W., 41, *113*
Milic, L.T., 49, 55, *113*
Minsky, M., 2, 3, 18, 23, 46, 49, 89, 93, 94, *113*
Morgan, J.L., 2, 10, 11, 20, 22, 27, 28, *111*
Moskovit, L., 10, *113*

N
Nash, S., *113*
Norman, D.A., 23, 33, *113*

P
Paducheva, E.V., *113*
Petofi, J.S., *113*
Postal, P.M., 33, *113*
Prideaux, G.D., *109*

R
Reddy, M., 10, *113*
Reinhart, T., 3, 13, 14, 18, 19, 21, *113*
Ritchie, G.D., *113*
Robbins, S.W., 60, *114*
Rochester, S.R., 29, 33, 36, *114*
Rosenschein, S.J., *112*
Rumelhart, D.E., 23, 25, 29, 33, *113, 114*

S
Sadock, J.M., 16, *114*
Sag, I., 3, 21, *111*
Sanford, A.J., 24, 26, 35, *111, 114*
Schank, R.L., 22, 23, 49, *114*
Schmidt, S.J., 3, 4, 45, 46, *114*
Sedelow, S.Y., 6, 49, 54, *114*
Sedelow, W.A., 6, 49, 54, *114*
Sengul, C.J., 21, 23, 25, *109*
Short, M.H., 18, *113*
Simmons, C., 9, *114*
Stanley, J.P., 42, 43, 46, 60, 104, *114*
Stein, G., *114*
Stenning, K., 24, *115*
Stewart, A.H., *115*
Stine, P.C., 105, *115*
Stoddard, S., 28, 98, 106, *115*
Stone, V.F., 8, 22, *115*
Stotsky, S., 10, *115*

T
Tannen, D., *115*
Thomas, L., 92, *115*
Thompson, S., 28, 43, *112, 115*
Thorndyke, P.W., *115*

V
Van, R.J., *112*
Van de Velde, R.G., *115*
Van Dijk, T.A., 9, *110*

W

Webber, B.L., 10, 11, 27, 29, 33, 35, 40, *115*
Wender, K.F., *115*
Weymouth, A.G., *112*
Widdowson, H.G., *115, 116*
Winograd, T., 6, *116*
Witte, S.P., 10, 21, *116*
Wolfe, S.J., 43, 60, *114*

Subject Index

A
Agent displacement cohesion, *see* Cohesion
Ambiguity in cohesion, *see* Reader/processor
Anaphora, *see* Cohesion properties
Anaphoric Hierarchy, Theory of, 25–26, 40, 69, 98
Atomism, *see* Reductionism

B
Bead-string model, *see* Reader processing
Bridging, *see* Reader processing

C
Cataphora, *see* Cohesion properties
Coherence, *see also* Cohesion
   definition of, 6, 13–14, 19–20
Cohesion
   and ambiguity, *see* Reader/processor, interpretation of ambiguity
   categories selected for analysis, 32–33, 96
      agent displacement, 33, 43–45
      definite article, 33–40
      pronoun, 32, 40–45
   and coherence, 13–14, 19–20; *see also* Coherence
   and comprehensibility, 20
   definition of, 1, 13–23, 96
   distance in, *see* Cohesion properties
   ellipsis in, 18
   empirical evidence for, 17–18, 30, 70; *see also* Numerical data
   inference in, 18, 28–29
   patterns of, *see* Patterns of cohesion in written texts
   relativeness of, 30, 61, 85–87, 100; *see also* Cohesion Index; Research hypotheses
   rhetorical functions of, 103; *see also* Writer/producer rhetorical strategies of
   semantic relationships in, 27, 33, 39; *see also* Connectivity Hypothesis
   and syntax, 17, 34
   and translation, 106
Cohesion components, *see also* Numerical data; Research hypotheses
   definition of, 17–18
   networks
      analogy to knowledge frames, 25; *see also* Knowledge frames
      graphic depiction of, 30, 68–69; *see also* Maps; Research hypotheses
   occurrence of cohesive elements, 57–59
   occurrence of nodes, 56–57
   occurrence of ties
      fulfilled, 57–59, 99
      unfulfilled, 28–29, 59–61, 70, 86–87, 99, 103
Cohesion index, 61–67; *see also* Cohesion; Cohesion properties; Numerical data
   summary cohesion index, 66–67
Cohesion properties
   directionality, 20–22, 28, 37–38, 70, 98
      anaphora, 21–22
      cataphora, 21–22
   distance, 20–21, 30, 32, 98; *see also* Cohesion index
   and synergism, 61
   and text unity, 101–102
   intersection of cohesion networks, 20, 23
   number of cohesive ties, 20–21, 30
   reentry of cohesion networks, 20, 22, 86, 97–98
   types of cohesion, 20, 23; *see also* Cohesion
Complexity Hypothesis, *see* Connectivity Hypothesis
Computer processing, *see also* Reader processing
   FORTRAN/PL-1 program
      functions of, 51

location data input, 49, 70; see also
   Numerical data
mapping, 68, 70; see also Maps
plot procedure, 51–52
sample text, 53
future analysis by, 95–96
serial processing and pattern-matching, 49
SNOBOL4 program
   characteristics of, 49, 52
   data generated, 51; see also Numerical
      data
   marking method, 50, 58
   program segment, 131
   sample text, 50
   summary statistics, 51
Conduit Metaphor, 10, 38
Conjoint Frequency Effect, 25, 35
Connectivity Hypothesis, 26–27, 35, 69, 98,
   100–101; see also Cohesion; Reader
   processing
   and Complexity Hypothesis, 26
Cooperative Principle, Grice's, 16, 35

D

Database, see also Physical text
   evaluation of, 93–95
   potential for, 46, 93–94
   selection of
      passages within printed texts, 47, 95
      physical texts, 45–47, 93–95
      text-types, 93–94; see also Text-types
Definite article cohesion, see Cohesion
Definiteness, see also Anaphoric Hierarchy,
   Theory of; Cohesion
   definite article cohesion, 33–38, 40
   definition of, 36–37, 40
   pronoun cohesion, 33–38, 40–41
Directionality in cohesion, see Cohesion
   properties
Distance in cohesion networks, see Cohesion
   properties

F

First Sentence Fallacy, 28, 35
Frames, see Knowledge frames
Fulfilled cohesion, see Cohesion components

I

Intersection of cohesion networks, see
   Cohesion properties
Item-collection models, 3, 49

K

Knowledge frames, see also Cohesion
   components; Reader processing
   components of, 24
   definition of, 23–25
   storage of information in, 25, 69, 98–100

M

Maps, 7–8, 72–84, 90; see also Patterns of
   cohesion in written texts
   functions of, 70–71, 89
   as graphic depiction of
      cohesion networks, 51–52, 70–71, 101;
         see also Cohesion Components
      texture, 30, 52, 91, 101; see also Texture
         in written texts
   and numerical data, 68, 85–88, 101–102;
      see also Numerical data
   visual observations of, 71, 85–89
Memory search, see Reader processing,
   information retrieval in
Mental model of text, see Reader/processor;
   Writer/producer
Methodology, see also Computer processing
   evaluation of, 93–96

N

Network Model, see Reader processing
Number of cohesive ties, see Cohesion
   properties
Numerical data, see also Cohesion
   components; Cohesion index; Maps
   descriptive statistics, 55–67, 100–101
   computer-generated, 55
   occurrence of cohesion data, 56–61
   regularities, 56–61
   relative cohesiveness data, 61–67, 100
   summary statistics, 55, 66–67

P

Patterns of cohesion in written texts, see also
   Maps; Texture in written texts
   definition of, 4, 6–9, 17, 54, 91
Philosophy and cohesion, 16
Physical text, 7, 9, 11, 93; see also Database;
   Text
Pragmatics and cohesion, 16
Problem space, 2–4, 30; see also Text
   exploration of, 49, 54

Pronoun cohesion, *see* Cohesion
Psychology and cohesion, 16

R

Reader/processor, *see also* Reader processing
  competence
    effecting knowledge frames, 24–25, 39, 103–104; *see also* Knowledge frames
    interpreting texts, 11, 27–29, 45, 47, 99
  expectations, 103–104
  input to
    knowledge-frames, 34–39
    mental model of text, 10–11, 23–29, 89, 96; *see also* Textual synergism
    texture, 89, 91
  interpretation of ambiguity, 29, 41–42
  interpretation of cohesion, 34–35, 89, 91, 96, 99; *see also* Cohesion; Cohesion components, occurrence of ties
    commonality/variability of, 37–40, 47
  interpretation of text, 9–12, 27–28; *see also* Text
    commonality/variability of, 97
  strategies, 20, 99–100, 104–105
Reader-subject
  selection of, 47–48
  and selection of database, 93
Reader processing, 10–12
  cohesion models of
    bead-string, 68–69; *see also* Computer processing
    network, 68–70
  complexity of, 70, 88–89, 106
  efficiency of, 89, 97–100, 103
  information retrieval in, 23–27, 33, 68–69, 96–99, 103; *see also* Knowledge frames
    bridging in, 28–29, 40
    pattern matching in, 89, 101; *see also* Patterns of cohesion in written texts
    maps of cohesive ties, 89, 91
    serial, 49–50, 68–69
  perception in
    coherence, 19
    cohesion, 27, 97, 102, 105–106
    reader input to, 23–29
    theories of, 23–27
Reductionism, 1–2, 7, 92–93
Reentry of cohesion networks, *see* Cohesion properties

Research hypotheses, 29–31, 55, 61, 70; *see also* Cohesion Index; Numerical data
  confirmation of, 56, 59, 67, 91

S

Statistical results, *see* Numerical data
Synergism, *see* Reader/Processor; Textual synergism; Texture in written texts
Syntactic marker, *see* Cohesion

T

Text, *see also* Physical text; Problem space
  components of, 1–2, 6, 9, 15, 48–49
  definition of, 9–12, 92; *see also* Reader/processor; Writer/producer
  dimensionality of, *see* Texture in written texts
  evaluation of text as process, 97–100; *see also* Reader/processor; Reader processing
  patterns of, *see* Patterns of cohesion in written texts
  and social milieu, 3–4, 10, 106
  standards for, 45, 71
  unity of, 1, 19, 61, 86, 98, 100, 102–103; *see also* Cohesion properties
Text theory, 3–4
Text-types, *see also* Maps; Numerical data
  selection of, 46–47
  standards for categorizing, 45, 66, 93–95
  variation in
    maps, 71, 85
    occurrences of cohesion components, 56–61
    relative cohesiveness, 63–67
Textual synergism, 30, 92, 97; *see also* Reader/processor; Texture in written texts
  definition of, 1
Texture in written texts, *see also* Maps; Patterns of cohesion in written texts; Text
  computer depiction of, 90
  definition of, 1–6, 30
  dimensionality of, 4–6, 8, 54, 91, 102
  empirical evidence for, *see* Cohesion; Numerical data
  maps of, 30, 70, 89–91, 102
  and pattern, 7, 8, 54, 91, 102
  and synergism, *see* Textual synergism

and text, 54, 106
uniqueness of, 89
Theoretical linguistics and cohesion, 15–16
Types of cohesion, *see* Cohesion properties

U

Unfulfilled cohesion, *see* Cohesion components

W

Writer/producer, *see also* Text
   input to mental model of text, 10–11, 17, 20–23, 40, 97–98, 102
   and production of text, 3, 10, 97
   rhetorical strategies of, 20–23, 85–88, 97–98, 100, 102–104
   risks in, 104